Tackle Riding

Tackle Riding

Lieut.-Colonel

C. E. G. HOPE

with revisions by
CAPTAIN E. HARTLEY EDWARDS
Editor of *Riding*

STANLEY PAUL, LONDON

Stanley Paul & Co Ltd
3 Fitzroy Square, London W1P 6JD

An imprint of the Hutchinson Publishing Group

London Melbourne Sydney Auckland
Wellington Johannesburg and agencies
throughout the world

First published 1959
Reprinted 1961, 1963, 1968, 1970, 1971
Revised edition 1975
Reprinted 1979

Printed in Great Britain by litho at The Anchor Press Ltd
and bound by Wm Brendon & Son Ltd
both of Tiptree, Essex

ISBN 0 09 124111 1

Contents

Illustrations

Preface

It is a mistake to be dogmatic about most human endeavours, not the least riding. There have been—and are—so many schools of thought about the art and practice of horsemanship that the would-be rider may well be forgiven for being bewildered and finally giving up the whole subject in despair so that he can go out for a nice quiet hack on a—nice quiet hack. It is the great achievement of the horse—not sufficiently recognized—that his great strength and general readiness to oblige have given most of these ideas and methods the cachet of success. So I will not claim that the methods of equestrian education described in this book are the *only* right ones or that the same results cannot be achieved just as well in other ways.

I do think, however, that the general principles enunciated in the following pages and the objects to be attained are common to all schools of thought, the most important being, in my estimation, the acquisition of a firm, balanced seat, independent of the reins. I do not believe that any real comfort or pleasure for horse and rider can be obtained apart from this, much less consistent success in national or international competitions, whether they be show jumping, horse trials, gymkhanas, polo or dressage. So the greater part of this book is given up to the basic training of both horse and rider, particularly the latter, which is a subject that tends to be neglected or slurred over in the more advanced works on equitation, for which this little book may perhaps be found to be a useful preparation.

Many people, books and horses have helped me at one time or another, but now I particularly want to thank Captain Edy Goldman and his excellent staff for many happy and instructive hours at his Cheshire Equestrian Centre, Holmes Chapel, for reading and criticizing the jumping section of this book and for providing the models and guinea pigs for many photographs. My thanks, too, to Charles Harris, F.I.H., for so many practical demonstrations of lungeing both horse and rider and of riding instruction, and for checking generally the equitational parts of the book, with many

9

helpful suggestions. Most of the good things here are theirs, the errors and omissions are mine.

Finally I must make grateful acknowledgement to the magazines *Light Horse* and *Pony* for the use of blocks and other published material.

C. E. G. HOPE

1

The Foundations

Riding on the Lunge

'There are no equestrian secrets withheld from the rider who has patiently and thoroughly mastered the technique of riding on the lunge. The principles of lunge-riding never alter and for riders wishing to get the maximum of physical and aesthetic values from equestrianism this form of exercise, intelligently carried out, is essential.'—Charles Harris in *Riding Technique in Pictures* by C. E. G. Hope and Charles Harris, F.I.H.

The foundation of good riding—by which I mean enjoyable and successful riding—is the acquisition of a deep, balanced, independent position in the saddle.

This will sound a platitude to many; I prefer to call it an axiom, or self-evident truth.

That elusive quality called 'hands'—ideally the perfectly balanced combination of psychological and physical contact between horse and rider—depends basically on the rider being able to stay on his horse without having to hold on to the reins.

Once he has achieved this he can explore and savour all the delicate exchanges of impressions and ideas—conversations really, in which the dominant partner or leader is the rider—which flow back and forth between man and horse—through the reins.[1]

---

[1] Certainly many people are naturally endowed, by conformation and character, with what one calls 'light hands'. Those with long flat thighs, for example, will find themselves automatically deeper in the saddle than those with short round ones; others will have a natural balance and sympathy with the horse, usually combined with absence of fear, which will enable them to control horses that would pull other riders all over the place. This does not invalidate our axiom, for the majority of people who ride have not these qualities and come in all shapes and sizes; for them the physical process of acquiring a deep balanced independent seat is essential. Those lucky ones mentioned above will be all the better horsemen and women for it—and their horses much happier.

The method of obtaining this independent seat is quite simply stated:

Riding without stirrups and reins

The method described below is *riding on the lunge*, based on the practice at the Spanish Court Riding School of Vienna, the last inheritors in Europe of the old classical tradition of the art and science of horsemanship as taught by the great French riding master, François de la Guérinière, in the first half of the eighteenth century.

Preparation

Psychological considerations are most important. In the first place the exercise must be voluntary. No civilian pupil can be forced to put himself or herself on a horse without reins or stirrups at the end of a lungeing rein.

Some preliminary riding is a good thing in order that the pupil can acquire some confidence and feel reasonably secure in the saddle.

In the case of children, ten years is the lowest age for riding on the lunge. Bareback riding on small ponies is an excellent preparation for lunge exercises, for it can develop balance, and produce those priceless qualities of confidence, fearlessness, and close physical contact with the animal. Its drawback is that it tends to encourage straphanging; though this can be prevented by the use of the neck-strap. Indeed, the neck-strap ought to be an invariable part of the gear for the mount of a beginner rider, young or old.

Preliminary Considerations

Check the gear. For the horse this is:

> Snaffle bridle, with a lunge cavesson over it.
>
> Reins knotted short enough to prevent them flapping or interfering with the horse's mouth. (Their presence gives confidence from the feeling that they are available in an emergency.)
>
> Side reins.
>
> Neck-strap.
>
> Saddle.
>
> Lungeing rein.

The lungeing rein should be attached to the front ring of the cavesson. Some people allow the rein to be attached to the side rings, to the back ring of a head-collar, or even to the ring of the snaffle bit, either to the inside one or through it to the outside one. This mode of attachment sets up all kinds of unnecessary strains on the mouth, head and neck; it also reduces control, in that the horse, if it so wishes, can turn away from the centre and get into a position to exert a direct pull on the lungeing rein. On the contrary, the action of the rein on the front of the nose-band brings the horse round to face the trainer.

The side reins should be very carefully adjusted to allow the horse to move with a stride of normal length, but at the same time prevent him turning his head to either side or increasing the length of his stride unduly, which would upset the balance and confidence of the rider.

The saddle should be a modern one, with a deep waist and high cantle, thus helping the rider to get down in the saddle. It should have well-forward cut flaps with knee rolls.

For the rider:

> Proper riding boots, if possible, for they give better support and grip to the rider. Alternatively, jodhpurs with leather strappings.

> Usual riding jacket, or jersey or shirt sleeves, according to the weather.

> Riding cap or bowler.

The horse, or pony. The mount should be:

> Quiet, rather on the sluggish side than the reverse, but it must go freely without constant encouragement.

> Comfortable in action with level, balanced gaits.

> Not too big for the age and size of the rider. (The pony used in the illustration [*see* Plate 2] is definitely on the fat side, but she had the overriding advantages of absolute steadiness, smoothness of movement, and being well-known to the rider. In the case of children, especially, it is all to the good if the lessons can be given on their own ponies, who will themselves benefit from the exercise.)

The place. The work should always be carried out in an enclosed space, preferably in a covered school. More often than not it will have to be done out of doors, in which case rail off an area which will give you a working circular manège with a diameter of about 12 yards. Site in a quiet corner of a field as far away from roads or gates as possible. The horse to be used should be made accustomed to this place before any riding is begun.

Pre-work action. Before the actual lesson begins the horse should be ridden on the lunge by the trainer himself for about ten minutes on both reins with the pupil watching. This enables the trainer to try the horse out first for suitability—specially necessary if it happens to be the pupil's own horse, prepares the horse itself for the work, and enables the pupil to see what is going to happen to him, how much and how little is required. The trainer should demonstrate the various exercises that can be done on the lunge. In the case of a pony a lightweight assistant or experienced pupil should ride under instructions from the trainer.

The trainer should explain to the pupil on the ground the objects and the range of lunge work, emphasizing that the pupil will not be asked to do anything for which he does not feel quite ready.

Length of lesson. For adult beginners the first lessons should never exceed 20 minutes, with an equal amount of work on each rein and rest periods. According to progress made the time can be increased to 30 minutes and then to 45 minutes. The longer the time that can be spent *comfortably and without tiring* the better. In this the pupil must be the judge, although the trainer should be able to assess his suitability for further progress by the consistency of his positions in the early stages. It is waste of time to let the pupil go bumping haphazardly with mistakes uncorrected.

With children the initial period should not be more than 10 minutes (5 minutes on each rein). It will give confidence to a complete beginner if the pony is held by the assistant for the work at the halt and led round a few times at the walk and trot before the pupil is left alone for the first time at the end of the lunge.

The rate of increase of the riding time will depend, in ordinary civilian conditions, on the amount of time a pupil can give to riding, whether he can ride every day, once a week, or even less. Riding daily, a normally fit person should work up to 40 minutes in a month or six weeks. Riding weekly it will obviously take him longer. Progress made and the results to be derived from it will always be limited by the time factor.

The instructor.

(i) He must be an expert with the lungeing rein, so that he can concentrate all his main attention on the rider, while never relaxing his watch on the horse or pony.

(ii) He must be quick to spot faults and able to rectify them. In many cases there must be a priority of correction, letting minor faults go while a major one is put right, but as a general principle no wrong movement or position should be allowed to go on unchecked. On the other hand a beginner should not be confused with too many commands and corrections.

(iii) He must know exactly what he wants to achieve (*a*) ultimately, and (*b*) in any particular lesson.

(iv) He must be able to assess quickly the limitations and possibilities of the pupil and set his target accordingly.

(v) In all lunge work the progress must be voluntary. Never *force* a pupil into any new position or exercise until he *feels* ready for it.

(vi) If the pupil appears to be tiring unduly, stop the lesson, no matter how short it has been.

(vii) Do not carry on any exercise too long, and perform every exercise on both reins, watching for the differences in execution which are bound to appear.

(viii) Preliminary work with stirrups is sometimes advocated. If it helps to give confidence at the beginning stirrups can be used—the instructor must use his discretion; but there is really little point in it, for the whole object of the exercise is to get the rider *down* in the saddle, which the use of stirrups will not do.

First Lessons on the Lunge

At the Halt. The instructor gives the pupil a leg up and allows her (I use the feminine pronoun because the illustrations [Plates 1–4] show girls as pupils) to settle into a natural position.

She should be relaxed, legs hanging down naturally and loosely, with no attempt at gripping; hands resting on the thighs, nowhere near the saddle.

The instructor should impress on the pupil that intensive gripping is not necessary for staying in the saddle; indeed, that it will prevent her getting well *down* into the saddle.

He can now start establishing a correct position.

(i) The pupil holds the pommel of the saddle lightly. This is for balance and security, and the establishing of confidence. 'Holding' does not mean clinging on like grim death, but being in light contact.

(ii) Gentle pressure of the knees forwards and the thigh muscles downwards, so that their inner surface lies flat against the saddle with as large an area of contact as possible. This will bring the knees into a firm but not excessive contact with the saddle just behind the knee rolls.

(iii) The lower leg now hangs vertically below the knees.

(iv) By bending the ankles the toes are raised and the heels pushed slightly back, so that the toes and the knees are in one vertical line, the heels slightly below the toes.

Here the instructor will watch carefully for any stiffness of the ankles or too tight gripping with the calves.

(v) The seat is pushed down into the lowest part of the saddle, so that there is at least a hand's breadth between it and the cantle.

(vi) Body will be upright, back straight and slightly hollowed; shoulders and hips square to the front and level; any dropping of one shoulder or the other means a dropping of the corresponding hip, which means the body is not squarely balanced in the saddle: the root of most of the troubles above, to be watched for and corrected at the beginning.

(vii) Waist and neck supple, head erect and looking to the front between the horse's ears.

(viii) Arms lightly touching the sides, flexed at the elbows, wrists and fingers supple.

Several minutes should be devoted to getting the position right. The pupil should relax and reassume the position several times, as a definite exercise.

All this time she is lightly holding the pommel. She may now be invited to reduce the contact to one finger only, until she is confident of keeping balance.

The next stage is to let go of the pommel altogether and place the hands in the position of holding the reins: forearms nearly horizontal, wrists straight but supple—no bracing or tensing—fingers flexed. The hands should be three or four inches apart, backs of the hands outwards, and everything about them free and flexible.

Repeat the various stages of this lesson several times, until the pupil's position is well fixed at the halt. Do it first with somebody at the horse's head, and then with the pupil alone at the end of the lunge.

Explain to the pupil exactly what you are doing at each stage and the objects of the various exercises; also invite the pupil to give her impressions and describe her sensations during the work.

The main faults to look for at this stage are:

Over-tenseness and excessive gripping with knees and calves.

Stiffness of the ankles, waist and shoulders, or, indeed, any other part.

Hollowing the back too much.

Round shoulders and crouching when holding the pommel of the saddle.

Lowering one or other of the hips and so not sitting straight in the saddle.

Looking down.

Lower leg too far back.

Body leaning back.

Tendency to let the toes droop.

Conversely an exaggerated position of the heels, too low, causing general stiffness of ankles and legs.

The aim is to get the pupil into an easy and relaxed position— *not a slack one.*

Physical Exercises. When the pupil has become fairly confident and the position satisfactory, the suppling and muscle-building exercises can be begun—still at the halt.

Hands on hips. The hands placed palms open over and round the hip bones, thumbs bracing the loins; elbows out and in the same plane as the body. This exercise helps to straighten the shoulders, encourages an upright position.

Arms folded behind the back. Each hand firmly clasps the opposite elbow. This can be used to correct any tendency to crouching, rounding the back, and slackness of the loins and stomach.

Arms stretching sideways. A balancing exercise, affecting the muscles of the back, chest and shoulders. It also enables the instructor to check the straightness of the pupil's position in the saddle.

17

Arms stretching upwards. An advanced exercise, which also helps to straighten the back and to correct crouching: but it is more usefully used as a test of the rider's progress, i.e. that she can carry it out without lifting herself out of the saddle.

Hands held touching at chest level and then flung outwards. Good for chest expansion and suppling of the shoulders. The movement must be quick and vigorous.

Arms swinging. (*a*) One arm at a time. (*b*) Both arms together. (*c*) Both arms alternately. These are progressive exercises which should be begun after the stretching exercises described above are performed correctly, without any shifting of the lower part of the body. They have the same effects as the previous exercises, only more so, and, if done smoothly and rhythmically, increase suppleness and improve balance.

Faults to look for are letting the arms drop from the horizontal, moving the head and neck, swinging the body up and out of the saddle, swinging the legs and letting the toes go down, letting the swinging arms turn the body from one side to the other.

Body turning sideways. With hands on hips, or with arms stretched sideways, the body is turned from the waist first to the left and then to the right. Shoulders must go with the body, the arms remaining all the time in the same vertical plane. The hips should not move but remain facing to the front. Do not let the pupil attempt to overdo this exercise, which has its principal effect on the waist and loins; be content with the minimum of movement, provided it is *correctly done*.

Head turning. This consists of turning the head slowly first to the left then back to the front; then to the right and back to the front. After practice, progress to turning the head the full half circle.

This exercise can be carried out with other exercises such as hips firm, arms stretching, where the body itself is not moving. Its object is to loosen and supple the muscles of the neck and to get rid of all stiffness there, which is inclined to communicate itself to the rest of the body.

It is a difficult exercise and should not be performed on the move until the rider has made good progress on the lunge and established a consistent and firm position in the saddle. More than six or seven turns will cause dizziness.

On the Move. When the pupil knows the above exercises and can do them correctly without upsetting her position in the saddle, work on the move can be started.

The sequence of the work follows that of the work at the halt, except that more time at the beginning will be given to the preliminary lessons. The essence of the work is the riding without stirrups and reins; the exercises are only additional aids to strengthening and confirming the seat and suppling up the whole body.

So we begin at the walk, the pupil holding the pommel of the saddle. The first tendency will be to grip the saddle more firmly for security, and the body will fall into a crouching position. Encourage the pupil to sit up and hold the saddle as lightly as possible; this will probably come with growing confidence. Once the position is correct, halt and start again, and repeat until the gripping tendency is overcome. Do this exercise on both reins, and be very patient. It can take up the whole of the first 10-minute lesson.

Then gradually encourage the pupil to progress to a finger-touch of the pommel, as at the halt, and from there to letting it go altogether and letting the hands lie down the sides in a relaxed position.

Turn now to the legs and hips. The legs will tend to start swinging with the movement of the horse or pony. There will also be a tendency, not so much at the halt as at the trot, for the inner leg to drop and also for the body to lean inwards, with a resultant collapsed hip. The correction of these tendencies at the outset is a basic physical exercise for the pupil; it is most important that the instructor should detect these early faults at once and correct them one at a time.

Now the pupil will be able to take up the position of holding the reins, which will help to straighten the body and shoulders. Repeat the sequence—holding the pommel, finger on pommel, hands by the sides, and hands holding the reins—several times at the walk.

Further Progress. The above exercises can now be repeated at the trot. Let the pupil choose her own time for letting go of the saddle.

The first reaction will probably be a tendency to be left behind, for the seat to slide to the back of the saddle and for the legs to go forward and up. The instructor should have forewarned the pupil, so that this tendency will be resisted, and overcome by using the pommel contact quickly, then letting go again, and so on, until the rider is firm in the saddle. Give frequent rests while obtaining this result.

19

This is the time when basic faults can be eradicated.

Begin each new lesson with about two minutes' revision of the previous exercises. After these initial elementary exercises, proceed to 'hands on hips' and 'hands folded behind the back'.

As before begin at the walk. At the trot, either the inner leg will drop lower than the outside one, or, in an attempt to counteract the centripetal forces, the pupil will put more weight on the outside and the outside leg will be lower than the inside one. The latter will be the more usual trouble, for the rider will feel herself to be falling outwards and will cling and grip with the inside leg to prevent it. The correction is to tell the pupil to press down with the inside leg. It is essential that, whatever the gait and pace, the body should be upright in the same vertical plane as the horse. See that the elbows are not bent back, and that the legs do not slip forward. The toe must always be directly below the point of the knee. Watch for any stiffness appearing at the ankles, back and neck.

Reactions will not be the same on both reins, which is why it is so essential for the work to be carried on *equally* on each rein. Most riders—and horses—prefer to work on the right rein, and, being stronger to that side, will tend to be stiffer and more jerky in their movements. It is up to the instructor to spot this and encourage the pupil to relax, by letting her jog round at the trot, first with the arms hanging down the sides and then with the hands in the position of holding the reins, without doing any other exercises.

The frequency of the exercises will depend largely on the disposition and progress of the pupil.

Ideally, a pupil should spend anything up to four months on this stage. It is the basic one, and it cannot be repeated too often that its object is to establish the correct position and balance of the body.

At the next stage the more advanced exercises, described above (arms, body, legs and head) can be carried out. These will develop the ease and freedom of the whole body on the horse, gradually strengthen all the muscles used in riding, and increase the independence of the rider in the saddle.

In the early stages the gaits should be limited to walk and trot, the latter a slow one, not too energetic. With progress the pace of the trot can be increased, and the canter introduced. At each new gait or pace the same problems will arise as have been pointed out above, but if the basic work has been done thoroughly they should be less and less marked.

The same horse or pony should be used in the early stages, but when the pupil is more advanced it is as well to change the horse from time to time, otherwise the rider will become set for one type of horse and movement only.

In the final stages of riding on the lunge other exercises can be introduced if required, more to test the degree of balance and independence obtained than for anything else; such as swinging the legs from the knee downwards, bending the body backwards or forwards.

These, however, should *not* be used as training exercises, for it is obvious that they will have the opposite effect to the one intended —to get the seat *down* into the saddle.

Conclusion. Riding on the lunge is not necessarily an isolated section of riding training. It can very well be carried on together with ordinary riding school work. In the early stages, when the lessons are short, it is a valuable preliminary to normal work with reins and stirrups.

The work described above is of course only applicable to individual instruction. One instructor, with two assistants might cope with two riders on the lunge but with no more. Where pupils are taken by rides the next best thing is to have an assistant as leader with the ride following behind without reins or stirrups. If the school mounts are properly trained, this can be quite effective, but the results can never be so complete as from riding on the lunge. However, it is better than nothing, and the same principles apply.

The Horse's First Lessons

The Programme

The great thing about training is to be systematic and progressive; you do not want a programme so much as a sequence of lessons, on the length of which you must be prepared to be quite flexible. Every animal presents its own educational problem and you must develop your work accordingly, giving more time to one subject, less to another, according to the pupil's aptitude. Above all you must be patient.

So the following outline of a sequence of training is just a framework to guide you in planning the education—or re-education—of your pony.

Stage 1

Handling: Introduction to the head collar. Leading round. (This stage begins in foalhood and should go on for a long time, until the young creature is thoroughly accustomed to human people—not only the trainer but everybody else too, to being touched, patted and stroked all over, to having its feet lifted, and is not afraid of strange sights and sounds. He can also learn obedience to the voice and to the restraining or compelling action of the lead rein. It is a basic stage, too often neglected or unintelligently carried out.)

Stage II

(Should not begin before 3 years old)

A. Introduction to the lunge. Snaffle bit and cavesson (warm the bit before putting it on, and rub sugar on it). Leading round on the lunge. Simple obedience lessons—'walk'—'trot'—'come here', etc.
Maximum length of lesson 20 minutes.

B. Going free on the lunge. Walk and trot. During this stage the pony can be saddled, and learn to do all the work with the saddle on, and with side reins.
Maximum length of lesson 30 minutes

C. Continue work on the lunge. Canter.
D. Backing. This should be done during the lungeing lessons, being content with simply mounting and dismounting.
Maximum length of lesson 45 minutes.

Stage III

A. Mounted work. Free forward movement. Walk in straight lines. Begin with an assistant leading, and the pony should continue to obey the voice and actions of the leader. Gradually replace these with the leg and rein aids.
Up to 3 years the maximum length of lesson 20 minutes.

B. Free forward movement at walk and trot. Flexion.
Maximum length of lesson 30 minutes.

C. Walk and trot. Suppling exercises on wide circles.
D. Suppling exercises on smaller circles and a variety of figures. Simple changes of direction. Jumping over small obstacles can begin in this stage.
Maximum length of lesson 45 minutes.

Stage IV

A. Canter. Continue suppling exercises. Changes of gaits.
B. Turn on the forehand. (This is really an exercise in the application of the aids and should not be overdone.)

C. Begin lateral work. Shoulder in. Jumping training continued in this and subsequent stages over gradually higher obstacles.

Maximum length of lesson 45 minutes.

Stage V

A. Continue lateral work. Half pass.

B. Turn on the haunches.

C. Rein back. (During all these stages the new lessons will be short at first, mixed with the work already done, and every lesson should begin with a few minutes' revision of the previous one.)

Maximum length of lesson 45 minutes.

Stage VI

Advanced work. Collection. Changes of leg at the canter. Depending on the age and aptitude of the pupil and the skill and ultimate objective of the trainer, this sequence may be covered in anything from six months to two years.

Teaching a Foal

The first thing to remember is that each foal is an individual with its own characteristics, its own virtues and vices, and its own way of looking at life, but basically it is a combination of curiosity and timidity. If you have had the foal from birth, the task of getting to know it is easier because you know its background. More likely you have got a foal from a sale or by some other means and know very little of its previous life or how it has been treated. Whatever its background it will most certainly be frightened and thoroughly disgusted with people and with life in general; it will probably be very lonely too.

So all your actions must be as quiet and soothing and unobtrusive as possible. When it arrives don't waste time trying to pet it but get it into a loose box or shed well spread with bedding, with water provided in a bucket which the foal cannot knock over, and some hay in a corner. Your next move will depend entirely on its reactions. If it appears friendly and unafraid, you can pat it and talk to it and fraternize in a quiet way, but don't overdo it. The great snag to avoid in dealing with foals is their getting too cheeky and domineering; a worse fault, I think, than being too frightened.

If, as is more likely, it is really frightened and fed up, don't attempt to touch it. Talk to it reassuringly and then leave it to its own devices for the night. It is a great help, of course, if there are other ponies or animals about the place that it can hear off-stage, as it were, but its most important need will be peace and quiet.

Leave it for the night; then, in the morning, before breakfast, go and see it. How quickly you can proceed depends on its mental condition: it may have got over its first fright—a good test is whether it has eaten anything or not—or it may still view the human race with grave suspicion and try to get as far away as possible from its representative—yourself. In either case do not make any advances. Go about the routine business of mucking out, changing the water, laying down some fresh hay, and so on, as if it were not there. When this has been done leave it while you have breakfast; after breakfast take a chair and book and sit in the stall with the foal; read the book and wait. It had better be an interesting book—because you may have to sit there some time; make it a comfortable chair, too!

This part of the programme may take anything from an hour to several daily sessions, but sooner or later curiosity will overcome fear and suspicion. The first good sign will be when the young creature starts to eat in your presence; it means that it is beginning to take you for granted. If it remains off its feed, the only thing to do is to tempt it with a feed of titbits—sugar, carrots, etc., mixed with a little bran and chaff.

When it does start to make an approach towards you do not be in too much of a hurry to respond; let it go about this delicate business of making your acquaintance in its own way, sniffing you, jumping away, coming back, going away for another think, then another sniff, until it really begins to feel that you are harmless. It is not a bad plan to get up then and leave it for a while to ponder over the whole situation; it might even miss your company.

Before long you will be able to touch it, gently stroking and patting its neck and back; don't try to play about with its head or ears yet. At this point you can introduce rewards into the treatment; once he has let you touch him, have a piece of sugar handy and offer it to him. But do not—repeat not—start giving it titbits every time you appear, for it will come to expect them and be annoyed if it does not get them; and it will express its annoyance by nipping and boxing at you with its feet, and you will have a cheeky foal on your hands, who will become a complete nuisance.

Very soon now you will be able to slip a halter on its head, and that is the all-important first preliminary phase of Stage I completed. You may have to be very patient indeed, but you can rest assured that the more time you spend over this the more you will save in the later stages of his training. As I have said before, nearly all the educational troubles with young ponies and horses can be traced to their first experiences of man.

Leading

We left the pupil with a halter on for the first time. The next stage is teaching it to lead. Start your lessons in an enclosed place where it is absolutely quiet, and with a wall or hedge on at least one side. To begin with, lead the pony up and down the track with the wall or hedge on one side of him, so that he cannot start swinging out. Lead from both sides, positioning yourself on the side away from the wall. It is useful to have an assistant to walk behind the pony to encourage him gently to go forward if he is inclined to hang back.

If he dashes forward and starts to dance about on the end of the leading rein, do not worry; go forward with him and let him work off his energy; then quietly get him back into position. Speak to him quietly but firmly all the time, telling him to be steady, not to be a silly ass, and so on. The moment he has calmed down have a soft word, a pat and, occasionally but not every time, a titbit for him. It is very important, I think, to use the voice as a sign of satisfaction with what he has done, as horses and ponies are susceptible to changes of tones and to changes in the mind of the trainer, and your voice is the quickest reaction to his good behaviour and so the one that he is most likely to remember. Mrs. Moyra Williams has shown in her book *Horse Psychology* that it is by no means certain that the horse always associates a reward with the right cause, mainly, I fancy, because it does not follow quickly enough on the cause.

About 20 minutes is long enough for each lesson. Once he leads quietly up and down on both reins, has learned to walk on, halt, walk, trot, and such simple gait changes, you can take him out into the open to get him used to every kind of object.

It should not be long before you can advance to Stage II. The first thing is the introduction to the bit. A simple snaffle bridle is required and a small-sized light snaffle bit, with preferably a rubber or vulcanite half-moon mouthpiece. Warm the mouthpiece first, and coat it with some sugar, so that the pony will associate it always with a nice taste. If the pony has been properly handled, he will be used to your opening his mouth and the sweet taste will make him put out his tongue, so the job should be easy. Don't attach the leading rein to the bit, but still lead him about for a little while with the leading rein on the head-collar. Then you can introduce the lunge cavesson—and definitely it will be money well spent to get a proper one, for you will have endless use for it and will have a chance of preserving the softness of the pony's mouth. The picture (Plate 5) shows the correct fitting of the bit and cavesson.

25

Some people like to put a mouthing bit into a young pony's mouth and leave it in for hours in the stable for it to play with. Personally, I do not think it serves any useful purpose which cannot be achieved by a proper sequence of training and riding with a seat independent of the reins.

First Lungeing Lesson

We have led the young pupil about and introduced him to bit and bridle and lunge cavesson (stage II, A, in the Training Programme.) At the end of this part of the programme we can get the pupil to the end of the lunge rein and start leading him round in circles. If he is very amenable, you can introduce him straight away to the saddle, as in the pictures. If you are not sure of him, leave it until later—there is no hard and fast rule. But it is a good thing to get him used to things on his back as soon as possible; start, perhaps with a blanket or numnah, kept in place with a surcingle and pads. This gives something to fix side reins on, which I think are a great help in early training. Properly adjusted, they act as a gentle restraint, especially if the pony starts to go too fast, and help to keep him on the right curve. The photograph shows about the right tension of the reins to allow a nice free head position; the reins are, of course, of equal length, but the pony in the photograph had turned her head slightly to the right, thus slackening the right rein and tightening the left one, which shows one effect of the side reins. Note again the fitting of the bit and cavesson.

The lungeing rein is about 25 feet long, and give the pony most of that as its radius; the wider the circle the better. When on a left circle, hold the rein in the left hand, slack end in the right (do *not* wind the rein round your hand or wrist), to move round in a very small circle with the pony, keeping just behind the pony's shoulder. (*See* Plates 5–6.)

Correct lungeing is nothing but commonsense, but beginners or children can get themselves into a mess if they try to do it single-handed and the pony plays up. So I strongly recommend having an assistant, as used to be taught at the Army equitation schools. The work now divides into stages, in the first of which the trainer is at the end of the lunge rein in the centre of the circle, and the assistant, *placed on the outside*, leads the pony round. Note in the picture (Plate 5) how everyone is relaxed. The trainer is standing quietly, holding the lunge rein lightly, letting it hang freely and loosely—but not floppily—between him and the pony. If it begins to flop it means that the assistant is not making a correct circle.

The assistant is holding a short leading rein, also attached to the cavesson, so that there are no confusing pulls on the pony's mouth. Note the position of her hands, the right close to the head, the left at her side holding the free end of the leading rein.

The pony is completely relaxed, perhaps wondering what it is all about and what is going to happen next, but not *worried*. She has already a saddle on her back. She is walking well and freely, with no tendency to rush away. During this period of leading round, the pony continues to learn the words of command—Walk—Halt—Trot—Come here—and learns to obey them. After 3 or 4 minutes on one rein, the pony is led into the centre up to the trainer, who makes much of her and rewards her, and then changes the rein. *All work* must be done equally on each rein, and not more than a few minutes without a change. A very few lessons should have the pony ready for the next advance.

A few words here about the function of the assistant will not come amiss.

When the assistant is leading the pony, for the first few lessons, he or she should start on the inside, holding the cheek-piece of the bridle; but there is no hard and fast rule about this. If the pony shows a tendency to turn away outwards, then the position should be on the outside; and, if the pony keeps wanting to come in and talk to the trainer, it is obviously inside. The assistant's job is very important, and it is essential that he should keep going at a level pace and keep rigidly to the radius of the circle. The assistant must keep his mouth shut and obey the commands of the trainer—that is, make the pony obey them. When the trainer says 'walk', he steps off quietly, giving the pony the 'office' to move by pressure on the bridle. When the trainer says 'halt', he stops quickly but not jerkily. He carries some corn or titbits with him to give an instant reward to the pony on obeying the commands.

Except when carrying out the commands of the trainer, or if the pony resists, by dragging back or rushing forward, the assistant should not interfere in any way with the movement of the pony.

Progress on the Lunge

We now come to phase B of Stage II. 'Going free on the lunge. Walk and trot. . . . ' If you have not already done so, you should now get a saddle on the pony's back, but, as I have said before, there is no harm in doing this much earlier, if the pony is amenable.

The first lessons of this phase will be a transition from leading to lungeing. Up to now, the trainer has been in the centre, holding the lunge rein while the assistant was leading the pony round from the *outside* of the circle; now the assistant changes her position to the *inside* and gradually moves away from the pony—a yard or so at a time—so that it begins to find itself on its own, being controlled by the trainer's voice and the whip. The assistant must be careful not to get ahead of the pony or drag it along; it is the trainer's job now to obtain and maintain free forward movement.

The pony's body should follow the curvature of the circumference of the circle, whose radius is the length of the lungeing rein, and it should be kept as upright as possible, especially at the walk.

Work at the lunge should be at the walk and trot and only three commands should be used: 'walk', 'trot', and 'halt'. The first should be given a low-pitched, drawling sound, the second rather more shrilly and sharply, with plenty of rolling of the 'r'—'trrrrot'—the third short and sharp. The trainer alone gives the orders, since it is to his control that the pony must learn to submit.

The trainer should generally keep moving with the pony on a very small circle, the lungeing rein held at the level of the elbow, in whichever hand is most convenient.

When the pony has learnt the words of command and become obedient to them, which may be after a varying number of lessons, the assistant can leave his position at the head. Instead he comes about midway between the trainer and the pony, and slightly behind it. He holds the lungeing whip and walks round with the pony. He *must not wave the whip about or show it to the pony*, except for the specific purpose of making him keep up to the required pace and on the limit of the radius.

Note in the picture (Plate 5) the positions of trainer and assistant and the handling of the whip. The pony has his ears cocked slightly back, paying attention to both the voice and the whip, and is learning to understand both without fearing either.

After a few circles at walk and trot the assistant brings the pony into the centre for petting and rewarding and then the rein is changed and the lesson is repeated. A very short time should suffice to have the pony going entirely free and alone on the end of the lungeing rein, which will be the subject of the next section.

The bringing of the pony into the centre for each change of rein is an important part of the routine. It makes a welcome break for the pony, keeps it interested, increases its confidence in the trainer and gives an opportunity to inspect the tack and make any adjustments that may be necessary. Make this inspection a careful one, for the immediate removal of a possible source of discomfort or pain will make all the difference to the pony's future progress. Now, also, you can start, during these halts, to teach the pony to stand square on all four legs at the halt, which is the basis of all movement and balance.

This is the time when you can lay the foundations of a good-moving obedient pony—or you can spoil it for life. You must strive to get the pony moving at all paces with rhythm and regularity *on both reins*. All ponies and horses seem to have a bias to one side or the other and, unless you correct it at the beginning, you end by getting a one-sided animal whose movements will be unfree and unbalanced. (For the gaits *see* page 54 *et seq*.) You must learn to know what you want to attain in the movement of the pony, otherwise you will never be sure of getting it.

All the time you must watch the pony's movements, to see that it does not start to lag behind or to rush on ahead with too long and uneven strides; in the former case encouragement with voice and whip—showing it or switching behind the pony's feet—should improve the rhythm and momentum; in the latter it is best to halt and start again. The fatal thing is to let the error go on.

Anticipation and Prevention

We have accomplished the transition from the pony being led by the assistant at the end of the lunge rein to its going free on its own on the full extent of the rein. The trainer was in the centre holding the rein while the assistant gradually left the pony and came into the centre, too. When this stage is reached it is time to change over roles.

So the pony is halted and brought into the centre to be rewarded and made much of, all this being another opportunity to teach obedience and to keep the pony calm.

Now the assistant stays in the centre with the lunge rein, and the trainer gets into position roughly midway between the pony and the assistant where he is best placed to watch the pony, anticipate trouble, prevent it if possible, or deal with it promptly if it occurs. Like the course of true love, the training of a young horse or pony never runs absolutely smoothly. There are bound to be misunderstandings, which only tact and prompt action will save from developing into open quarrels. The great thing in training is to avoid a quarrel!

That is why I advocate the trainer having an assistant, especially for beginners. The expert can manage a horse single-handed but the beginner may only get into trouble.

The assistant's job is to keep the lungeing rein at a reasonable tension and to obey the orders of the trainer, who is now responsible for the control of movement and pace. When the change-over first takes place the trainer should lead the pony back to the circumference of the circle and lead it round quietly once, talking to it so as to reassure it that nothing very terrible is going to happen when it is left alone at the end of the rein. The trainer should carry his whip with him, letting it hang or drag casually behind him, so that the pony becomes aware of its presence. Let me emphasize here that the whip is not a weapon of punishment but part of the equipment of instruction, an aid which will be replaced in due course by the legs of the rider. If the trainer is intelligent and sensitive, he will find this little private promenade with his pupil invaluable, discovering whether the pony walks along freely and confidently, or is nervous, or lazy, or just awaiting a chance to be naughty. Then he slips away to a position half-way between the pony and the centre and slightly to the rear.

If the pony stops he should show it the whip, which will normally be sufficient; if not, then a touch on the hocks accompanied by the command to 'walk on' will get it moving. If the pony turns inward, go forward towards it, talking to it softly but firmly, and turn it back on to the circle.

Do not retreat from the pony when it plays up, but take the initiative immediately so that it has no chance of getting out of control.

Get the pony trotting on the circle as soon as possible. It may get excited and rush round at a furious rate. Do not check it immediately because free forward movement is what you are aiming at; here again the voice will help to calm it down, and the assistant must gently vibrate the lungeing rein. Once it has done a couple of circles at a quiet steady trot, slow down to a walk, halt and bring it into the centre for the usual reward and to change the rein.

I cannot exaggerate the importance of this business of bringing the pony into the centre, making less and less use of the lunge rein to pull it in and more and more use of the voice. The habit of obedience instilled in it now will stand you in good stead when you are wanting to catch it in a field on a cold morning.

I must emphasize once again the necessity for proper equipment. If you cannot afford a proper cavesson, it is possible to make a substitute by getting a ring stitched to the front of the head-collar. Above all, avoid any kind of short cut to control that involves a noose or slip-knot over the pony's head or through its mouth.

Backing

If the training described in the last few pages has been properly carried out, with tact and gentle firmness, the next stage—backing—should present no difficulties. You have already lunged the pony with a saddle on his back and applied gentle hand pressure, so that he should be more than half prepared for what is coming.

Begin the mounting day with a lunge lesson, just as if it were a normal training session that he is used to; try to forget about yourself and not get excited or nervous. Do nothing different this day, but make sure that you have a feed bowl immediately to hand, and an extra assistant, who should have been on the scene for two or three previous lessons.

After working off his superfluous energy on the lunge, bring the pupil quietly into the centre and *relax*.

One assistant is at the pony's head with the feed bowl; the other stands by while the trainer adjusts the saddle and repeats the hand pressure and pattings of previous lessons. The pony is quite relaxed, standing well, and deeply interested in the feed bowl. The moment is propitious for the next stage—raising the rider not more than half-way across the saddle, then quickly and quietly down again.

After repeating this a few times, the trainer lifts the rider higher over the saddle. At first the rider should stay passive, lying across the saddle. The other assistant concentrates on the pony, not letting herself be distracted by watching the rider. If her attention should wander, so may the pony's from the feed bowl, and that is when troubles begin.

Once the pony accepts this, the rider is lowered and then raised across the saddle so that the full weight is now on the pony's back. The rider now can pat the pony's flanks and generally make much of it.

The pupil, having behaved well in the first stages of mounting, we can now complete the operation. We have now come to Stage III of the programme—free forward movement, first with an assistant leading the pony in a straight line.

The trainer now lifts the assistant completely over the pony's back and on to the saddle. The assistant moves about in the saddle and pats the pony, while the trainer moves up to the pony's head to distract its attention. If there is any doubt of the pony's reactions, this operation can be repeated once or twice. In any case it helps to get the pony used to movement on its back. If all goes well, the second assistant quietly turns and leads the pony forward, and it moves for the first time with a rider on its back. Once the pony shows no

31

tendency to slow down, stop, or arch its back, the leader quietly drops back level with the shoulder and allows the pony to go forward on its own, the leading rein being held close as a precaution. This is the beginning of free forward movement.

The object all through has been to bring the pony forward steadily and to overcome resistances and disobediences by forestalling them and by careful, gentle but firm preliminary training. The first requirement of the trainer is patience. There are quicker ways of breaking in ponies and horses, but for children and beginners the longer way is the soundest; indeed, I think, in the long run, it is the best method in all circumstances, especially for ponies. Being by nature more intelligent and self-willed than horses, they can the more easily be spoiled by bad and hurried training, as the many letters I receive prove only too clearly.

Balancing Exercises

When the pupil has made progress on the lunge and has been backed, whether as a new boy or on a refresher course, you can start giving him mounted balancing exercises.

Mark out an area of 40 yd. × 20 yd. Stones or posts at the corners and half and quarter markers will be sufficient.

Start off by simply 'going large' at the walk as in Fig. 1 (1). The arrows indicate the diagonals for change of rein. Keep a steady, even pace with strides of equal length and regular rhythm. Count to yourself: 'One—two—three—four. One—two—three—four,' and use your legs gently to keep the pony moving level. In this way you will achieve rhythm and cadence—mysterious words which only mean what I have described.[1]

Make as exact a half circle at each end of the school as you can, and keep yourself and the pony upright. Don't let him fall inwards, which is a common tendency. A fault the rider should avoid is a tendency to lower the outside leg and lean over that way. You should have somebody on foot to tell you when you and/or the pony are falling from the vertical.

When you feel all right at the walk, repeat at the trot. Try to go as smoothly as possible from walk to trot, and once again keep a steady pace and even rhythm—'One—two. One—two,' this time. If you are re-training a horse or pony, finish off the lesson with a canter; with a new pupil, keep to the trot for a few days. When

[1] *Cadence :* The normal and natural sequence of footfalls to each stride. *Rhythm :* The weight stress on each foot during a complete stride. *Tempo :* Miles per hour, or the speed. (Definitions by Charles Harris, *Light Horse*, February 1955.)

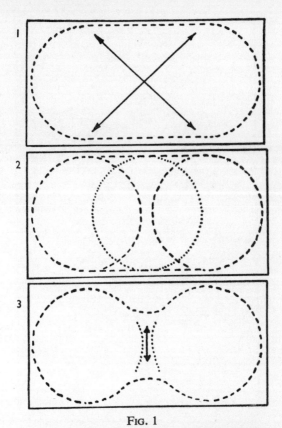

FIG. 1

The diagrams are reproduced from *Equitation Notes*
by Charles Harris, F.I.H., published in LIGHT HORSE

changing direction at the canter always carry out a simple change of
leg.

Work on each rein equally at each gait. The daily lesson should
last no longer than half an hour. Work for one week on each
diagram.

The second week you begin to close in the circles, as in Fig. 1 (2).
These are 20-yard circles, which you have already prepared for by
doing the half circles for the first week. Circle at each end of the
school first, until you thoroughly get the feel of the figure, then try

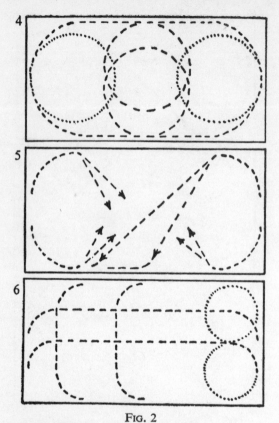

FIG. 2

The diagrams are reproduced from *Equitation Notes* by Charles Harris, F.I.H., published in LIGHT HORSE

the centre circle, without the sides and ends of the school to guide you. You can do endless variations on this simple basic theme. When you want to change the rein go large and then change the diagonal.

Once again watch the rhythm of the gaits very carefully, get into the habit of counting—out loud if you like, as that rhythmical noise might help the horse to regulate his own stride. Once again, also, see that you remain upright.

For the third week, here is a simple 'from-the-wall-to-the-wall' exercise [Fig. 1 (3)], which you can mix in with the figures of the previous week. Now you can practise the change of rein from one circle to the other, but always see that you do the same amount of work on each rein.

Up to now the work has been done at the ordinary gaits—walk, trot and canter. For 10-yard circles at the trot and canter, however, you must change to collected or slow gaits. (*See* page 69.) If the pupil is not well trained, just try and make it a slower gait, by raising his head a little and shortening his stride. Don't forget the outside rein in this work, otherwise your pony will swing his quarters out. Maintain a consistent pace at the direct turns, not letting your pony slow down or quicken his pace as he comes to them. Vary the point at which you make the turn, or else your pony will start anticipating you. (See Fig. 2.)

The fourth exercise in our series introduces you to the 15-yard circle, the variations of and transitions to which are clearly marked on the diagram. Carry out these circles at each end first before attempting them in the middle of the school. [Fig. 2 (4)]

In number five we have more variations on the original theme. From your half circle begin with the short diagonal change, which gives you half the length of the long side of the school to steady up. When this change is done smoothly, then do the long diagonal. [Fig. 2 (5).]

The sixth exercise brings you to the 10-yard circle, which is best done at the corners of the school as shown in the diagram. This is blended with quarter circles and straight line work across the school and away from the sides. [Fig. 2 (6).]

The essence of these exercises is steadiness and regularity; do not be tempted to go ahead too fast. Watch your own position all the time.

The gaits to be used are the ordinary walk, trot and canter. Each gait should be steady and level, but on no account slack and sloppy. Do not attempt collected gaits beyond the extent mentioned above; these can come later, when the fundamental balance and control have been achieved. Always begin each lesson with a quick refresher of the exercises already done. This prepares the pony— and yourself—for the new and more difficult movements to come, and ensures that you have consolidated the early lessons before proceeding to the new.

Pay great attention to keeping upright. The pony's body should bend on the arc of the circle, but should not tend to fall inwards, which is a natural reaction to the centrifugal force produced by making a circle. You must counteract it by the inside leg and outside rein, and by the uprightness of your own body in the saddle.

Be sure to maintain the pace and rhythm of movement on the circles. Don't let the pony slow down or swing his quarters out on the circle. If you have the facilities, it would help to mark out a whitewash circle at each of the required diameters; if that is not feasible, a centre line down the school and side markers at 10-yard intervals will guide you well.

2

Control and Guidance

'Two fundamental principles of control and guidance are: first, to *know* what you want the horse to do, and second, to *prepare* and *place* the horse correctly for carrying out the movement.'—*Riding Technique in Pictures*, by C. E. G. Hope and Charles Harris, F.I.H.

Mounting and Dismounting

From observation, the technique of getting on to the back of a horse is one sadly neglected in most places of instruction.

First impressions are always important, and the attainment of smoothness, suppleness and rhythm in all riding work, which has been stressed already, should be extended to the preliminaries of riding as much as to the actual process itself. The first impressions of a horse, as a heavy, ungainly weight heaves and bangs and scrambles and—nearly always—jerks the reins and so the bit in the mouth before finally landing with a bump in the saddle, can hardly be pleasant ones. No wonder so many horses and ponies are fidgety when being mounted. Is it possible, I wonder, that much of the troubles riders experience with their horses and ponies spring from this first awkward contact?

I wouldn't know. But there is no reason why a horseman should not learn, and practise, a smooth, elegant, and tactful way of mounting.

Begin by approaching your horse, whether a strange one or your old friend, quietly and from the side. There is a blind spot directly in front of the horse's eyes, and he is always apt to be disturbed by something he cannot see.

Take hold of the bridle with a pat on the neck and a quiet word or two. The voice can play a far greater part in the training and controlling of a horse than it is often allowed to do.

Now Inspect the Equipment

It is surprising how many apparently experienced riders get caught across country, in the jumping ring, or any other awkward time with a broken rein, stirrup leather or girth.

The basic cause of this is taking your saddlery for granted, forgetting that things wear out.

Every riding instructor worth the name should impress upon his or her pupils from the very beginning the necessity for inspecting tack carefully before mounting.

It should become a routine, the instructor setting the example.

Look at the Bridle

Does it fit?

Are the cheek pieces the right length?

Are they the same length either side?

Is the brow-band clear of the ears?

Is the nose-band in the right position, about two fingers' depth below the cheek bones?

Can you get two fingers between it and the horse's face?

Is the throat latch too loose? Or too tight? You should be able to get the flat of your hand comfortably between it and the jaw.

Is the bit correctly placed in the mouth? Not too high and pinching the corners of the mouth. Not too low and rattling against the teeth.

Is the curb chain (with a curb bit, double bridle, pelham, etc.) twisted so that the links lie flat in the chin groove when activated?

Is the stitching of straps all in order, especially at buckles, if they are used?

Look at the Girths

Are the straps and buckles, both on the girths and on the saddle firm, with all stitching in order?

Is there any sign of wear in the straps?

Are they nice and soft? Or hard, brittle—and dangerous?

Are they properly adjusted so that there is no wrinkling of the skin under them, likely to lead to a gall? Run your fingers down between the girth and the skin. Are they tight enough?

Look at the Stirrup Leathers

Are they worn or cracked? Especially at the buckles, at the D's of the saddle and where they go through the irons.

Check that the thumbpiece on the stirrup bar is in the down position. Do not ride with the thumbpiece closed.

Is the stitching at the buckles in order?

Look at the Saddle

Is it on right? Not too far forward so that the withers are pinched. Nor too far back, throwing weight on the loins.

Is the tree in order, i.e. the pommel, which should be just behind the point of the wither, has a good clearance above the wither, with no sign of spreading.

Flaps soft and pliable.

No grease or polish on the seat of the saddle.

Padding firm and sufficient.

Look at any other gear that may be on the horse: martingale-breastplate, crupper, and so forth.[1]

Quite a lot to look at when enumerated in detail like this! It may take two or three minutes before you mount. What are three minutes on the ground compared with eternity under it?

Actually this quiet pause before you mount may be very beneficial in calming a fidgety horse. The calm, methodical procedure of the human being cannot fail to impress itself on the naturally impressionable mind of the horse.

People advocate checking the length of the stirrup leathers before you mount; an approximate guide is the length of your arm. But it will have to be checked again when you have mounted.

Meanwhile, it can make mounting much easier if you let the near side leather down several holes.

Mounting

(a) **From a Mounting Block.** To the young and energetic this may sound effete and decadent! In the horse age mounting blocks abounded in public streets, together with hitching posts; and it is undoubtedly the most comfortable way of getting mounted—for the horse, too! It is also good for young children, better than hoisting them up, in that it is always better for a beginner to do things for himself than to have them done for him.

---

[1] Crupper or breastplate is sometimes necessary on small ponies to keep the saddle in place.

I would recommend every stable to have a mounting block, and to train all ponies to stand quietly beside it. It all helps to make them steadier for mounting on other occasions.

You can either put your foot in the stirrup first, or the outside leg over first.

(b) **The Leg-Up.** This is not so easy as it looks ! How many riders have found themselves thrown over the other side of the horse by an energetic 'legger-up'? It is equally disconcerting not to be hoisted high enough. The technique is as follows:

Positions. The rider stands facing the saddle, left hand holding the reins[1] and the neck in front of the withers; or the pommel if you prefer it.

The assistant stands directly behind the rider and close to him or her.

The rider lifts his or her left leg so that it is horizontal from the knee downwards.

The assistant cups the knee with his left hand and holds the ankle with his right.

Hoisting. The rider gives the signal; the assistant gives a controlled lift, smoothly and without violence, high enough to

[1] *Holding the reins.* This seems the right moment for describing the *holding* of the reins but not their *functions* which will be discussed later. Common sense is always the guide, the method being adapted to the work to be done. The normal method, as recommended by the Pony Club—and therefore to be used if you want to pass the various tests—is as follows:

Single rein—in one hand. Left rein outside little finger; right rein between first and second fingers, with the slack of the rein across the palm and between the first finger and thumb. Alternatively the right rein can be held between the first finger and thumb; in which case the end of the right rein passes downwards across the palm and under the little finger, and the end of the left rein goes in the reverse direction and between the first finger and thumb. This method seems to give more flexible control when riding with one hand, e.g. playing polo or in gymkhana events, with less chance of the reins slipping.

Single rein—in each hand. From the above position, slip the little finger of the right hand inside the right rein and draw the reins apart, securing the respective ends between the respective first fingers and thumbs. Some people prefer to have the reins between the third and little fingers.

Double rein—in one hand. The positioning is as follows:

40

enable the rider's right leg to clear the horse's croup; the rider assists by springing lightly off the right foot.

If correctly done, the rider's left knee makes immediate contact with the saddle.

It is worth practising this, because you never know when you may not be called upon to give a leg up. It has not been unknown for both rider and assistant to concentrate on the wrong leg!

Like everything else to do with equitation, practise on both sides of the horse.

(c) **Mounting With Stirrups.** Whether somebody holds the horse or not, the technique is the same.

(i) Reins in the left hand, in the correct positions between the fingers. (*See footnote, page* 40.)

(ii) Rider's body is level with the horse's shoulder, turned slightly to the rear.

(iii) Left hand on the neck in front of the wither, or on the pommel. The rein contact should be even (unless the horse is fidgety and inclined to turn away, in which case shorten the left rein).

(iv) Take the stirrup in the right hand and place the foot in the stirrup, with the toe well down so that it does not

Left snaffle rein *outside* the little finger.
Left curb rein *between* little and third fingers.
Right curb rein *between* the second and first fingers.
Right snaffle rein *outside* the first finger.
The free ends are held between first finger and thumb.
Alternatively, the right reins can be held so that the curb rein is between the second and third fingers and the snaffle rein between the first and second fingers.

Double Rein—in each hand. From the above position, insert the little finger of the right hand between the two right reins and draw them apart. As before the free ends are held between the respective first fingers and thumbs.

Some people place the curb rein on the outside and the snaffle rein inside. It all depends on the horse—and the rider. In a competition test, you may want the horse to flex his mouth and play with his bit and it may be more effective to have the curb rein outside and a shade shorter than the snaffle rein. When schooling a horse, it is sometimes useful to hold the curb reins in one hand and the snaffle reins in the other, giving great flexibility of control.

41

stick into the horse's side, thereby encouraging him to move away.

(v) With the foot safely in the stirrup, take hold of the waist or cantle of the saddle with the right hand.

(vi) Left knee against the saddle flap, and spring from the right foot, pressing left toe well down and away from the horse's side.

(vii) The body is momentarily upright, supported by the left foot in the stirrup and hands on the wither and saddle.

(viii) Swing the right leg well over the saddle, keeping it clear of the croup, and shift right hand to the pommel.

(ix) Support yourself with the left foot and hands and lower yourself *quietly* into the saddle.

Do not come down with a bump: it only disturbs the horse and your own position and balance.

(x) Put your right foot into the stirrup without looking down and adjust the reins. (*See footnote, page* 40.)

Do not move forward immediately, remain quite relaxed without any leg pressure and with light feeling of the bit. The horse should understand that mounting is *not* an automatic signal to go on.

In any kind of competition, whether gymkhana, show jumping or horse trials—and certainly out hunting— a horse trained to stand still when being mounted will be a godsend to you and worth many points.

This operation has been broken up into its component parts as a guide to instructors and for those who are really keen to learn the fundamentals of horsemanship and to do things the right way. There are instructors who will consider this is a waste of time; they are the type who will allow young pupils to go out riding, even on main roads, without proper headgear.

All mounting instruction should be carried out on both sides of the horse.

(*d*) **Mounting Without Stirrups.** This is a physical exercise, which requires some strength and practice. Except on to very small ponies, young children should not be asked to mount without stirrups.

With reins held fairly tight in the left hand, face the horse opposite the saddle, left hand on neck or pommel, right hand on waist or cantle.

Spring up smartly from both feet and pull up with the arms, until the body is straight, supported by the now straightened arms.

Swing the right leg over the saddle, as when mounting with stirrups, and shift the right hand to the pommel.

As before, take great care to land quietly.

As before, do not let the horse move off at once.

(*e*) **Vaulting.** This again is very good physical exercise for adults, but not generally recommended for children.

Stand facing towards the horse's head and neck, with both hands on the pommel. Swing the right leg forwards, then sharply back, and with forearms and back muscles swing the body backwards and up, over the saddle.

This exercise is of course much easier when done on the move and is one of the basic *voltige* movements learned by trick riders in the circus.

The technique is to run with the horse, holding on to the saddle pommel or hand grips on either side of the wither, body facing forward and level with the withers. Jump *forward*, so that you land with both feet on the ground and *ahead* of the horse's wither and fore-legs and make the spring from there, which will land you correctly. If you try to do it from level with the wither, you will be left behind. The whole process is very well described in *Trick-riding and Voltige*, translated by Antony Hippisley-Coxe from the Dutch of H. J. Lijsen (published by J. A. Allen).

Mounting this way should not be done without expert super-vision, but ability to do so would no doubt be of great value in gymkhana events.

(*f*) **Dismounting.** The safest and quickest way is to take your feet out of the stirrups, and quickly swing the right leg over the horse's back and land facing the horse with both feet on the ground together.

Do take care to swing the leg high so that it does not touch the croup.

Don't let go of the reins.

The Riding Position. (Plate 7). There are many riding positions, adapted over the years for specialist jobs, the overriding qualifica-tions in every case being comfort and efficiency.

The cowboy or gaucho would be very unhappy if he had to sit like a jockey for eight hours a day and longer rounding up cattle; the jockey would get nowhere if he rode like a man hunting hounds; the show jumper or cross-country rider has to modify his position in order to ride adequately in a dressage test. And the saddles for all these activities vary too.

In these days when specialization has been carried further than ever before in the search for maximum efficiency—and may well go further still—there is no such thing as an *all*-purpose seat. There is, however, I suggest, a *starting point*, a basic position from which any specialized activity can be developed.

This is the balanced independent seat which has already been described in the section on 'Riding on the lunge'. It can fairly be called an axiom that the less a rider relies on the reins to keep him in position on the back of a horse the better rider he will be and the happier his horse.

Certainly many riders get to the top of the tree—or very near it—without much basic training at all: especially in show jumping. These usually start with natural gifts of balance and physical conformation—and then they have the horse. Let us not forget the horse; and give credit where credit is due.

The strength and docility of the horse are such that he can get himself and his rider out of all sorts of incipient trouble and make it look as if the rider has done it all himself. The ultimate result, from the rider's point of view, is effective and successful, but it is seldom artistic or scientific, nor good riding.

The basic riding position has already been described (pages 16 and 17) for the rider on the lunge without reins or stirrups. Whether the pupil has done any lunge work or not the same principles will apply.

The trainer should get the pupil into the saddle quietly, preferably from a mounting block or with a leg-up, and make her settle herself down in the saddle without reins or stirrups.

Then adjust the stirrups to the required length, and check the rider's position again. It should be:

Easy and supple.

Body upright, back gently braced but not stiff.

Head erect, eyes to the front.

Neck supple.

Forearms, wrists and hands follow the line of the reins.

Fingers flexible, making a light contact through the reins with the horse's mouth.

44

Backs of the hands may face either downwards or upwards (I do not mean horizontally up or down, but a tendency in either direction). Generally there is more lightness if the palms of the hands face upwards, and the fingers play with the reins; but riders vary, and also situations vary, so that the position of the hands must be constantly changing to suit the requirements of the situation and the moods of the horse. *The thing to avoid like poison is rigidity.* The term I do not like is the 'fixed hand'. It means something, but requires explaining to most riders, beginners or otherwise, and is far too often interpreted in practice as a rigid hand, which in the end will make a horse lean on his bit—the most common fault in any dressage competition today.

Seat is in the lowest part of the saddle.

Knees, thighs and calves in light contact with the saddle.

The area of contact with the saddle should be as great as possible. Too great pressure with the calves and little or none with the knees leads to a weak and unbalanced seat, and stiffness lower down at the ankles and feet. The grease marks and signs of wear on your boots or jodhpurs will show whether you are in the habit of sitting correctly or not. The signs should be more or less evenly distributed all the way up the *inside* and not showing along the back.

Ankles supple. *See also above.*

Heels down and toes up. There should be no undue pressing down of the heels, which creates a stiff unnatural position, easily recognizable by the strained attitude of the rider generally. The knee and ankle joints should be very supple, so that the lower legs can move freely and independently for the application of the aids or signals to the horse.

Hands and Reins

Rein action. The reins can act in an almost infinite variety of ways. Their function is to support the action of the legs and to clarify or amplify the signals given by them. For instance, if the legs tell the horse to go forward, the action of the right rein can give it the further instruction to turn to the right. That is the combined action of the legs and reins in its simplest form.

The reins are, of course, merely a connecting link between the rider's hands and the horse's mouth, which in their turn are the interpreters from the human brain to the equine one of the thoughts, wishes and emotions of the rider. It is important to remember this last thing. The hands will not only transmit commands to the horse, they will reveal to it his rider's feelings, nerves, fear, anger, pleasure—it all gets through and affects the horse in some way or other; which is why the temperament of the rider is such an important factor in horse training and riding, and why patience and self-control are so necessary and so continually dinned into the ears of pupils by instructors and writers of books down the ages. 'The golden rule,' wrote Xenophon twenty-two centuries ago, 'in dealing with a horse is never to approach him angrily'; no one has bettered that advice since.

For the word 'reins' we will now substitute 'hands'.

The hands have three functions:

They can *act*.

They can *resist*.

They can *yield*.

They *act* when they increase the tension on the reins, when they invite—or compel—the horse to flex his mouth, bend his neck in order to reduce speed, change direction, stop, and rein back. Through the bit the hands act on the mouth, the head and neck, and the shoulders, and indirectly on the hindquarters.

They act indirectly, or in opposition, when the rein on the opposite side to the required direction of movement is laid against the horse's neck or wither.

This indirect action is used in neck-reining a horse, when only one hand can be used, as in polo, cattle drafting, gymkhanas and similar activities. A horse responsive to neck-reining is said to be bridle wise.

There is an almost infinite variety of application of these actions to the needs of both rider and horse. The more experienced the rider becomes, the more educated the horse or pony, the more subtle will these actions and reactions become in their turn. It is all a matter of feeling and what has been called 'equestrian tact'.

Legs

However much the protagonists of forward and collected schools of riding may disagree, they are all united in stressing the paramount importance of the rider's legs in successful equitation.

Without going into complicated mechanics, it is clear that, while the head and neck play an important part in movement and a strong,

46

long neck and sloping shoulders are essential for optimum results, the original source of forward movement, whether on the flat or into the air, come from the hindquarters of the horse. The longer and stronger are the muscles of the thighs, that is from the hip to the point of the hock, the more powerful will be the impulsion, giving length of stride and speed. As a matter of interest, Crepello, winner of the 1957 Derby, measured 44 inches from hip to hock, a tremendous length in proportion to his height of 16.0½ h.h. Ballymoss, who was beaten by a length and a half in that race, standing 15.3½ h.h., had a measurement of 38½ inches. Length by itself is not decisive, equally necessary being right proportions and quality of muscle. However, it is quite a good guide when first looking at a horse to consider that distance from hip to hock.

The legs of the rider, correctly used, bring into action the latent power of the horse's hindquarters, activating the muscles and making the hindlegs engage well under the horse, which has, amongst other things, the effect of lightening the forehand and shifting backwards the centre of gravity.

The legs should be in contact with the horse all the way down from knee to calf. Additional contact is obtained when necessary by the moving inwards and slightly backwards of the heels, so that they can touch the horse's flanks behind the girth. Spurs, without rowels, should be regarded as a refinement to be lightly used to reduce the amount of actual leg action. They should never be worn by a beginner rider or in the initial stages of training.

A sensitive intelligent horse will seldom need a spur, whereas a coarse, thick-skinned animal, including many a pony, will be all the better for a spur; even so this should be sparingly used, for horses and ponies quickly become hardened to all these things. Once again it is a question of equestrian tact which can seldom be taught but only acquired.

The rider should be able to apply the legs together, or singly, in combination with the action of the hands but independent of it. This power of independent action can only be acquired by hard work in the early stages of riding, preferably by lessons on the lunge as I have described in Chapter 1, and plenty of physical exercises.

Let not the week-end rider or the child at school despair! All the exercises that have been described can be done on a wooden horse, balustrade, saddle stand, branch of a tree, or anything over which you can put a leg. In addition, let me recommend skipping as a first-rate preparation for riding and for strengthening and suppling the thigh, calf and back muscles.

With the leg action there is also back action; the muscles of the back, especially at the loins and hips, come into play in almost everything you do and they act in unison with the leg muscles in riding more or less unconsciously and to a greater or less degree according to the effort made. Like every other muscle they can be trained and exercised and tuned up so that they will have the greatest possible effect without becoming stiff. Do not confuse the back muscles with those of the seat; the former have a downwards effect, the latter tend to squeeze the body up and out of the saddle.

Bits, Bridles and Saddles

All bits are variations of two basic types:

    A. Snaffle.

    B. Curb.

A. The *snaffle* consists of a mouthpiece, usually jointed, and two rings to take the cheek-pieces of the bridle and the reins.

When the reins are used directly and straight back it acts on the corners of the lips, and has the effect of raising the horse's head. If the reins are held low and tight there is a nutcracker action of the two parts of the jointed mouthpiece on the sides of the lower lips and tongue.

The successful use of the snaffle goes with a strong, independent seat, the rider's hands being used to guide and control and not to preserve his own balance. Used in combination with a weak seat the action can be very severe, usually producing a hard or dead mouth and a tendency for the horse to lean on the bit.

For schooling horses with sensitive or tender mouths, or who are afraid to face the bit, a milder variant is the snaffle with a straight or half-moon mouthpiece, made of metal, rubber, vulcanite or nylon. Modern bits with either rubber or nylon mouths are reinforced through the centre so that there is no likelihood of the bit breaking when in use.

When used by itself, not in combination with a curb bit, the mouthpiece should be as thick as possible without making it too heavy. The side rings should be large, as in the 'egg-butt' and 'D' varieties. Leather or rubber side guards give extra protection to the sensitive corners of the lips, preventing them from being pinched between the rings and the mouthpiece.

So long as transitions of pace are gradual, i.e. that the horse is not asked to change too quickly from a faster to a slower pace the snaffle is the ideal all-round bit; all preliminary training should be carried out with it, and all novice riding.

When gadgets such as dropped nose-bands, gags, martingales, and so forth become necessary it means that the mouth has become spoiled through hasty or inefficient schooling, through strap-hanging, and excessive pulling about of the mouth. The true answer for these troubles is re-schooling.

B. The *curb* consists of two bars each divided into two parts—a short upper arm to which is attached the cheek-piece of the bridle, and a longer lower arm to which is attached the rein. Dividing these two parts is the mouthpiece, which usually has a slightly curved centre (port) to accommodate the horse's tongue and prevent it from seeking freedom over the bit. On the rings of the upper arms are hooks from which hangs the curb chain.

When the direct rein action is exerted the end of the lower arm comes back, the whole bar pivoting round the mouthpiece. The upper arm goes forward exerting slight pressure on the poll via the cheek-pieces of the bridle and, more strongly, causing the curb chain to move into and press against the chin groove, the hollow of soft skin at the back of the horse's jaw above the chin.

The curb chain should come effectively into action when the lower bar of the bit is at an angle of about 45 degrees from the vertical. If the bit is too high in the mouth the rein action will cause the curb chain to be raised too high when it will act against the thinly covered bone above the chin groove, with the worst possible results. A lip strap holding the chain to the lower arms helps to keep it in its proper position.

The spectacle, all too common, of the curb bit horizontal means that either the bit is badly fitted, the curb chain is too loose, the whole bit is the wrong size for the horse's mouth, or a combination of all these causes.

The strength and effectiveness of the curb bit varies with the length of the lower arm and of course with the way it is used.

As with the snaffle its ideal use goes with a strong seat. Weak riding and strap-hanging can do even more damage to the horse's mouth than they do with a snaffle. It is essential that the horse should be ridden in a curb with the lightest of contacts; when extra force has to be used, it should only be for very short periods, e.g. sharply and suddenly as when stopping at polo, and immediately relaxed.

In normal riding the curb is seldom used by itself, but in combination with the snaffle (double bridle). In experienced hands this combination can produce every desired result from basic riding to high school.

A useful variation of the curb is the Pelham, which combines the snaffle and curb actions in one bit. The same principles apply to the handling of the reins, and it is a practical bit for small ponies or for horses which will not take kindly to a double bridle.

A very common sight is a Pelham bit with a single double-ended rein. This enables a child to hold a single rein, but the varying and subtle effects of snaffle and curb actions are completely lost in one general effect. Its use is neither logical nor sensible.

Bridles

The bit is attached to a bridle, which consists basically of two cheek-pieces going over the top of the head, held in place by a brow-band and a throat latch (pronounced *lash*). The nose-band, which hangs also from the top of the head and is usually placed a little over midway between the eyes and the nostrils, is really only a decoration —unless of course it is used for the attachment of a standing martingale.

If two bits are used then it becomes a double bridle, with two sets of cheek-pieces. (Plate 7.) Any saddler's catalogue will supply the details.

The drop nose-band was invented by the Germans and was much used in the German cavalry. Its first use was as a corrective to certain bad habits such as shaking and tossing the head, getting the tongue over the bit, opening the mouth too wide. Its prevalent use in this country as a stopper—by restricting the breathing—is a grievous act of cruelty and the negation of all training.

To be correctly fitted for its proper use (Plate 7) the front half of the nose-band should lie a hand's breadth above the nostrils; the rear half hangs practically at right angles to the front part, in front of the rings of the snaffle bit, over the mouthpiece and behind the jaw. It can be used with a running martingale to correct excessively high head carriage. It is of course only used with a snaffle bit.

Its effect can be increased by tightening, but the front part should never be allowed to hang low over the nostrils, where it becomes a refined instrument of torture. Combined with a standing martingale it is the negation of all horsemanship and training.

At polo, when everything happens at a furious pace and there is no time for the niceties of manège work, a horse's head almost inevitably tends to get too high—it is part of the training of a polo pony to raise its head—and a standing martingale then becomes a necessity. Provided it is not too tight and attached to an ordinary nose-band, I have known it do little harm to most polo ponies, who never needed it in ordinary riding, exercise or hacking.

The running martingale is attached to the girth, like the standing variety, but the other end is bifurcated, with rings through which go the reins. If intelligently and tactfully used, it corrects head raising tendencies, especially in show jumping competitions, where again there is little time for subtle hand and rein actions. When used with a double bridle the martingale rings should pass over the curb rein.

The Saddle

The art of the saddle-maker has done much to perpetuate what is known as the English hunting seat. The low cantle and straight flaps encouraged a backward and armchair position.

It has taken a long time for the saddler to catch up with the modern principles of jumping and produce a saddle based on a sprung tree, as opposed to the traditional rigid wood and metal foundation. Piero Santini produced the first modern show-jumping saddle in Italy between the wars; the French were early in the field too, notably with the Danloux saddle; since then various types have appeared—Pariani, Toptani, Barnsby and the like, all of which have their supporters.

The main features of all these saddles are the deep waist and high cantle, the forward-cut flaps with knee rolls, and, in the case of the Danloux, supports in the rear behind the thighs of the rider. The effect is to help the rider to achieve first of all a deep central position in the saddle and then to keep forward and with the movement of the horse.

Saddles on the same lines are now made for dressage riding and also for both uses. The lower picture on Plate 7 shows the salient features of an all-purposes saddle and its effect on the rider's position. The saddle used by the rider on the same page is a conventional British show saddle; the straight flap can be seen and the low cantle compared with the modern version below.

About the Aids

It is customary in most books on riding to describe various actions of hands and legs which will produce certain desired reactions in the horse or pony—or not. These are quite correct and helpful, but they represent as it were a general convention of language—a sort of 'Oxford or B.B.C. accent'—which is applicable to well-educated animals. But there are innumerable dialects in the language of the aids, and so you have to apply the principles intelligently to particular cases. What cannot happen is that the aids you might be given for, say, a canter pirouette will be translated correctly by a pony that has not yet learnt to turn correctly on its haunches.

'Definitive aids can never be laid down as they vary day to day and stage by stage as rider and horse progress in their training.'[1]

However, it is useful to know the general language, so I will describe the conventional aids and how they should be applied.

The first and most important aid, which must always be applied before any of the others mentioned below, is the mind and the will of the rider. Before you ask your pony to do anything you must see the action in your mind's eye—in other words you must know as much as possible of all that is involved even in a simple action like walking—and you must make up your mind that he is going to do it.

In the case of the walk from the halt, what do you want the pony to do? Obviously to alert him and make him move forward, preferably with a hind foot first. What do you do? Stimulate the hindquarters—which is where propulsion and forward movement come from—with the only instrument available—your legs. According to the state of training and nature of the mount the action of the legs may be anything from a gentle, firm, and equal pressure of both legs to a good bang of the heels. The latter is not artistic, but it is what so many children have to do to their ponies to make them move at all! It is after all only an emphatic version of the polite 'B.B.C. accent', the 'gentle pressure' so loved by instructors.

Well, you have woken him up and he is ready to go forward. What happens next? The pony won't go forward unless there is no obstacle to prevent him; in this case the bit and your hands controlling it through the reins. So you stop that hanging on to the mouth and give him the freedom to go forward. And off you go. If you thought about it in this way, you could give the accepted aids for the walk from the halt without ever being told what they are, namely:

Extra pressure with both legs evenly; let the head go forward by easing the reins.

You will find, especially if you have done a lot of riding on the lunge as described in Chapter 1, that the muscles of your back will come, more or less instinctively, into play when driving the pony forward—the more so if some extra effort is needed with a sluggish pony; they will force your seat down into the saddle, in extreme cases move it backwards and forwards in a driving movement which undoubtedly plays its part in obtaining the desired result, namely, to make your pony start walking forward.

To stop, all you do is to increase the pressure of the legs, but hold your hands still, i.e. do not yield. You thus send the pony forward on to the bit, which this time does not yield, so his normal

[1] *Riding Technique in Pictures*, by C. E. G. Hope and Charles Harris.

reaction is to stop. There is no necessity to move the body at all, beyond bringing your shoulders slightly to the rear of your hips, which, by placing more weight on the quarters, will assist the process of slowing down.

Normally, you should always bring your pony down to the walk before halting. The action for decreasing pace and for descending from a faster gait to a slower, e.g. canter to trot, is the same as for the halt. The moment the transition is made, let the hands yield a little, so that the pony understands to go on at the new gait, i.e. gallop to canter, canter to trot, trot to walk. In advanced training you teach the pony to stop and start at any gait, and ultimately, as in polo, a pony is taught to stop from a full gallop. But this is a long way ahead!

It is well to remember that it is not, as so often stated, the action of the seat muscles that brings about these effects—their action is to squeeze the body out of the saddle not down into it, but of the muscles of the back, from which all your own actions and movements start. The more you can use your legs and not your hands to control your pony the better it will go. And this is the way to success in gymkhana events, which are becoming very important these days.

I have taken a long time to describe a simple action, but it is really fundamental to a proper understanding of the aids and so to good riding. It will be noticed that we have so far only used the reins *directly*.

3

Movement

The Halt

The halt is the starting point of movement. In a good halt position all the potentiality of the horse for future action should be poised in latent impulsion, obtained by the legs and hands of the rider. A straddling extended position with the quarters and hocks left behind means a loss of efficiency and quickness in starting.

A properly united and balanced position gives the horse control over all his limbs and the power to move off smoothly into any direction at any gait.

'At the halt,' say the F.E.I. Rules, 'the horse should stand attentive, motionless and straight with the weight evenly distributed over all four legs and be ready to move off at the slightest indication of the rider. The neck raised, the poll high, the head a little in front of the vertical, the mouth light, the horse champing his bit and maintaining a light contact with his rider's hand.'

The training of the horse to stand correctly can begin with the first work on the lunge. Every time the horse is brought into the centre, it can be encouraged to stand quiet and square on all four legs. The trainer will watch the hindlegs particularly, for the weight of the forehand generally will induce the correct position in front, whereas the horse is inclined to extend himself to the rear and to rest one or other hindfoot. The trainer will be content with a comfortable, easy position at this stage, without trying to get the hindlegs under the horse. Forcing a horse into an extreme position before his muscles are ready for it will only provoke resistance and create stiffness.

The correct position of the halt is when the forelegs and the hindlegs from the points of the hocks downwards are absolutely vertical. Any deviation, forwards in the case of the forelegs and backwards in the case of the hindlegs, is a bad fault. Bunching, the reverse deviation, is generally due to exaggerated collection imposed too soon.

Both these faults can be avoided by early lessons on the ground.

In all schooling the rider should remember to bring his horse to a correct halt before beginning any moving exercise. The more this is practised the easier will be all the subsequent work.

At this stage it is necessary to examine briefly the movements of the horse.

The Walk

The horse walks in what is called four-time, which means that four clear and distinct hoof beats (cadence) are required, in a consistent, even succession (rhythm). The hindfoot should step beyond, or into, the track of the forefoot, not behind it. The walk is one of the more difficult gaits to maintain correctly; the tendency is for either the lateral or diagonal pairs to draw together. The latter produces a jerky, uneven gait; the former produces the amble or pace, which was much used by riders who had to cover long distances. There is nothing so comfortable as a horse with a long, striding, level walk.

> 'The beauty of the walk is marked by length, freedom, evenness and lightness of stride, each one of the four steps comprising a complete stride fully contributing to the balance of the gait.'
> (Charles Harris, *Light Horse*, June, 1953).

Many disappointments in training are due to lack of appreciation of the mechanics of movement and consequent development of faulty and unbalanced action, hence the importance of balancing exercises, such as I have described in Chapter 1.

Near.	Phase 1 ●	●	Phase 2 ○	○	Phase 3 ● ●	Phase 4 ○
Off.	(Elementary)	●			(Elementary) ●	○

Near.	Phase 5	●	Phase 6	Phase 7	●	Phase 8 ○
Off	(Elementary) ●	●	○ ○	(Elementary) ● ●		○

The table above shows eight phases of the walk to each complete stride. The dots show the sequence of footfalls—black indicate the most marked beats of the gait, white the intermediate phases. This applies also to the tables for trot, canter, and gallop. There are many variations within each phase, but these represent the main stages of a walk stride.

The Trot

The trot is called a two-time gait in which the fore and hind pairs of limbs follow each other almost—but not quite—together, either diagonally (off fore—near hind, near fore—off hind) or laterally (off fore—off hind, near fore—near hind). In fact the footfalls follow in succession, although so close together in their pairs that only high-speed photography can detect it, as the sequence opposite shows. There is an instant of complete suspension between each diagonal when all four feet are in the air. This was known to the ancient Egyptians but only proved in 1882 by Muybridge's photography.

The trot is the lightest and most balanced of all the gaits of the horse, and can be the most spectacular.

The F.E.I. recognize three variations of the trot, ordinary trot, collected trot, extended trot, the differences between which need not concern us at present. Proper training on the lunge will help to set the trot gaits, but after that your own riding will make or mar it.

The first consideration is to be able to sit as still as possible, which you can only do if your legs and body are in the right position, and you have acquired the right balance and feel of the motion of the animal beneath you, so that you go *with* it all the time. So long as your body balance is right you will not need to use the reins to keep on correcting it and to catch up with the movement of the pony.

Then you must sit absolutely straight, with square hips and supple back. If you get slack and let one hip or the other drop, your weight will tend to fall sideways, which will affect the balance of your pony at once, the result being an uneven stride, with one diagonal shorter than the other.

Thirdly, when you rise at the trot, go up as little as possible. All you need is to get your seat just off the saddle and lightly down again. If you do this correctly, you can apply your leg aids just as effectively from a rising trot as from a sitting one. What is more, you will look much better doing it, and you will find the pony going much better, too. Remember, of course, always to change the diagonal at regular intervals, especially when schooling or on a long ride.

The great fault in trotting is to become a one-diagonal rider. This is one of the causes of one-sidedness in horses and ponies. The trot is a beautiful gait, at its best light, balanced, and brilliant, but it can easily be spoilt by bad training and bad riding.

Near.	Phase 1 ●	Phase 2	Phase 3	Phase 4
Off.	(Elementary) ●	O	(Elementary)	O
Near.	Phase 5 ●	Phase 6 O	Phase 7	Phase 8 O
Off.	(Elementary) ●		(Elementary)	

Table showing eight phases of one complete trot stride.

The Canter

A good canter is the most beautiful of all the horse's movements. To ride it well is not so easy as it seems to be at first sight; to go perfectly with the movement and not roll from side to side with swinging legs requires strong deep and supple seat, entirely independent of the reins.

The canter is a three-time gait, which differs from the trot through the breaking of the beat of one of the diagonal pairs, so that you get the leading fore and hindlegs which gives the gait its impulsion and characteristic rhythm.

The officially recognized (F.E.I.) variations of the canter are collected, ordinary and extended, and the approximate lengths of stride in each case, for a horse, are 5 feet, 8 feet, and 12 feet.

The job of the rider is to feel the rhythm of movement clearly under him, and the test of your ability to ride the canter correctly is whether you can feel which leg is leading without looking down. Properly done the canter can be the most artistically satisfying—for the onlooker as well as the rider—of all the gaits.

The rider who has been correctly trained from the beginning and has developed a deep independent seat will sit upright and show as little movement as possible, the body supple but not loose. There should be no rising and falling as in the riding trot, which gives you a sack-of-potatoes appearance, and also tends to produce a rolling gait in the horse. The essence of the canter is a flowing forward movement, rather like the rhythm of an incoming wave, with as little sideways displacement as possible.

When riding across country, especially when the ground is uneven or undulating, a more forward position is desirable, because you must keep your centre of gravity level with that of the horse, thus obviously giving the greatest mechanical freedom of movement.

The important thing is to avoid unnecessary movement in the saddle, especially that rise and fall, which I have mentioned above—and is so often seen. Each foreleg takes the whole combined weight

57

of horse and rider at every other stride, which at a 12-m.p.h. canter is roughly 1½ times every second. Even if you sit still there is strain enough on the fetlock joints and pasterns; why add to it by unnecessary movement and bumping about?

Near.	Phase 1 Period of	Phase 2 (Elementary)	Phase 3		Phase 4 O	
Off.	complete suspension	●	O	O	O	O

Near.	Phase 5 ●	Phase 6 O O	Phase 7 O O	Phase 8 ●
Off.	(Elementary) ●	O		

The eight basic phases of a complete canter stride.

The Gallop

The gallop is one of the true natural gaits of the horse. In the wild state it was his main defence against his enemies. Fear is the great stimulator of the gallop, as anybody who has sat on a real runaway will at once appreciate.

The rhythm of the gallop differs from that of the canter. It can be recognized by having a break in time which splits the sequence of the diagonal pair of legs when cantering, which gives the gallop a leaping effect from the two hindlegs on to the two forelegs. This was translated by old artists into the spread-out position so familiar in sporting prints before the days of photography. When a horse is tired or temporarily off balance the horse develops a rotary sequence of the legs, a sort of rolling gait.

The length of gallop of an ordinary, fit and reasonably well-trained horse is approximately 15 to 20 feet. A well-balanced thoroughbred will make a stride of from 20 feet upwards, this depending also on its breeding.

The position of the rider in the gallop should be well forward so that his centre of gravity and that of the horse are one. Correct balance is very important in the gallop, especially where extreme speeds are required, and the various positions used by riders when hunting, playing polo, and racing have a considerable effect on the gait and speed.

As in everything else, the acquirement of the correct gallop depends on correct early training; on a consistent balance being established by work on the lunge, and on the building up of muscle, which will enable the horse to use himself with the maximum of freedom.

A good gallop is enjoyed by every horse and pony and rider, but too much of it will break down even the fittest horse. On the other hand, more fast work would do most dressage horses a great deal of good, if only as a relaxation from their ordinary work. The great rider James Fillis believed wholeheartedly in this; some of his best horses, incidentally, were ex-racehorses.

Near.	Phase 1 (Elementary)	Phase 2	O	Phase 3	●	Phase 4	O
Off.	●		O	(Elementary)			O
Near.	Phase 5	Phase 6	O	Phase 7	●		
Off.	(Elementary) ●		O	(Elementary)			

Eight basic phases of the gallop stride.

English is the only language which has separate words for the faster gaits of the horse—canter and gallop. On the continent the word 'gallop' covers all the varieties of the gait, often leading to some confusion.

So far as the human control of the horse is concerned, the object of the gallop is to obtain the greatest possible speed for a given distance regardless of all other considerations. The gallop gait, like everything else, can be made or marred by early training, and great care should be taken in early training on the lunge and mounted to give full freedom to the head and neck, so that a head-in-air, hollow-backed action is avoided.

When training a horse to gallop, mounted, develop the first gallop slowly from the canter—you should know from this same study of the mechanics when the horse passes to the gallop gait from the canter. Keep at a slow gallop for some time until the horse moves freely and well within himself. Then progress to short bursts of high speed.

The aid from the gallop is simply strong pressure of the legs with a marked but not heavy contact with the mouth, the hands tending to go forward with and steadying the movement. This contact will vary with the type of horse and the use of the gallop. The racehorse needs a very strong contact; on the other hand, a polo pony or gymkhana pony should learn to go at the fastest possible pace with a loose rein. To reduce the pace and to drop down to a slower gait, keep contact with the legs and 'fix' your hands—that is, do not let them give to the movement. If the horse does not respond immediately, a sharp jerk may be necessary; but avoid a steady, heavy pull on the reins, which ends by making the horse lean on the bit.

When training a horse for galloping events, the great thing is to keep a balance between the basic slow work, walking and trotting, which builds up the muscles and strengthens the lungs, and actual galloping. If a horse or pony has too little galloping, he will be out of practice and will never reach his full speed; on the other hand, if you over-gallop him, he may break down. For ordinary purposes a distance of 100 yards full out twice a day in the later stages of training should be ample. Regular short sharp bursts like this will probably improve a nappy or over-exuberant pony, for it releases a lot of surplus energy. But keep the galloping spells even shorter until about a fortnight before the event you are training for.

The position of the rider can affect the ease and speed of the gallop, and there is no doubt that the best position is well forward.

4

The Aids Applied

Transitions

We can now resume our discussion of the aids and their application. The jargon of dressage test riding has given the word 'transition' a rather esoteric significance, but it is only the change from one gait to another. All riding is a matter of transition. Transitions from slow to faster gaits are *upward*; from fast to slower gaits *downward*.

I want to amplify a little what I wrote about the basic aid for forward movement. First we concentrated on getting into a walk from the halt. The essence of that was leg action and a slight yielding of the hands. Now we want to think some more about this business of 'yielding'. The stronger the rider and the better trained the horse the wider and more subtle can become the range of effect of this action. In its simplest form, the horse will know from the amount of give exactly how fast the rider wants the next gait to be; what should never happen is that on being told to move off the horse (or pony) should immediately get into *his*—usually the fastest—pace. This usually happens when the reins are allowed to go slack at the same time as the legs are applied, and is why we see so many ponies get out of control the moment they are asked to go into a faster gait.

Moreover, you want all your changes of gait—transitions, we call them—to be as smooth and light as possible; it not only looks better but feels better. You also want to be sure that the pony will go off at the pace *you* have decided, instead of *him* deciding on his own—in the absence of any definite instruction from you.

So practise these simple transitions in the school and you will find the pullers, that so many have trouble with, being gradually transformed. By 'school' I mean any enclosed space—a field with some hurdles set up to mark out an area of about 40 by 20 yards, or as near to that as you can get, or a few posts and ropes, or even corner and centre markers—where it is quiet and the pony cannot get away.

Walk round the school once or twice, then make a large circle of half the school; the pony at attention and striding out evenly and at a steady consistent pace. When you are ready apply your legs but do *not* relax the reins. This is not a contradiction of what was said (page 52) about 'yielding' but a common sense adaptation of the principle for practical purposes. Too often, as I have said, 'yielding' means a loose rein and an out-of-control pony; the finer shades will follow as you gain experience. For the present, make your pony break into a trot without altering the tension on the reins. (Plate 8.) This does *not* mean *pulling* on the reins, nor setting your hands rigidly; all the time you should be gently playing with your fingers on the pony's mouth. The pony will break into a controlled trot and will keep that pace so long as you maintain the same rein and leg contact. After two or three circles ease your legs, maintaining the same rein contact and let the pony drop down softly into a walk. Make much of him. Repeat that several times, then change the rein and repeat the process on the other rein. Vary the exercise by going round the whole of the school—'going large'—and by circles in the other half of the school. After about twenty minutes have a rest, and let the pony walk round the school on a loose rein.

Trot to Canter

The transition from the trot to the canter is produced in the same way basically as the transition from walk to trot. The basic principle is that the pony must move off at *your* pace, and not his, and that you keep contact with his mouth and not let the reins go slack. There is an important difference, however, in that when moving from the trot to the canter you change the rhythm as well as the speed.

The movement of the canter has already been described; briefly, it is a change from a two-time gait to a three-time, the pony moving as it were by bounds rather than in a steady one-two, one-two movement.

If you want to strike off at a canter with, say, the off fore leading, you want to consider these objects: (1) to keep the pony in a straight line and not moving in two tracks; (2) to have his head bent slightly to the right; (3) to take the weight off the right foot so as to allow it to strike forward in the leading phase of the canter; (4) to maintain the necessary impulsion from the quarters, and (5) to prevent him from rushing off at excessive speed in this—to him—exciting new gait.

To prevent No. 5 happening, you make the general contact with the mouth as I have already described; to obtain No. 4 you continue to act with your legs—which may mean anything from a steady pressure (with a well-trained pony) to a series of bangs on the flanks with your heels (with the lazy 'old soldier'). Nos. 2 and 3 effects are obtained by the action of the right rein moving across to the left just in front of the withers (having an indirect action) combined with the yielding slightly of the left rein. No. 1—the tendency to swing the quarters to the left—will be counteracted by extra pressure of the left leg and a shifting of the body weight to the left. You will find then that you have used diagonal aids, the right rein (indirect rein of opposition) and the left leg. (Plate 9.)

When learning these aids, or teaching them to your pony, you should always start on a circle, preferably within one half of the manège. Avoid looking down at the start of the canter, or at any time during the movement; it only upsets the balance of yourself and your mount. Until you acquire a sensitiveness to the movement of the horse get somebody standing on the ground to tell you whether he is cantering right or wrong.

Changing Direction

The next important thing is to change direction on the move. The foundation of this is the exercise called 'from the wall (or track) to the wall (or track)'. It is simply a slight deviation from the straight line along the side of the school and back again; if this is done correctly, then everything else will follow in due time.

The pictures (Plate 10) show exactly what I mean. In the top picture a ride of adults is performing this movement. Note the poles laid parallel beside the track as a guide.

In the next picture, the rider, a child, is riding alone. The length of the poles gives the distance to be covered off the track, to which the rider returns directly afterwards.

The pony seems to have got a little excited about this new exercise, but the rider is taking him nice and quietly on a gentle diagonal away from the side, using the right leg and the left rein. The aid need be very slight, more a yielding of the right rein than a pulling of the left. The actual giving with the left rein and so lightening the contact on that side has the effect of emphasizing the effect of the right rein. Extra pressure of the right leg supports and supplements this emphasis and the pony moves off the straight at a very gradual angle. At the instant when the change is begun, the pony is in the position for the movement known as shoulder-in, a very important part of advanced schooling. So you see all this careful preparation

63

is getting you somewhere! To bring the pony back to the track you reverse the aids already given.

Circles

We dealt with circles in the section on training the young horse (balancing exercises), when we stressed the need for keeping upright. To keep upright on a curve you must be able to use your legs firmly—the inside one to keep the horse from falling inwards, the outside one to prevent a swinging outwards of the hindquarters. Watch your own position, that you do not lower the outside leg and lean over away from the movement. When circling, the pony's hind legs must follow the front legs, so that the foot-prints of the one coincide with those of the other. All changes of direction (other than by lateral movement) involve going on a circle for a shorter or greater distance. The sharper the turn the shorter the arc. The secret of all aids is to prepare the horse for them a little in advance of where a particular movement is required, so that he has some inkling of what is going to happen and is not taken by surprise at the last minute by a sudden jerk on the rein or a kick in the ribs. (Of course, out of doors when hacking or hunting, you don't always know what is going to happen yourself, but if the training in the school has been done correctly, that will not matter.) So, before you come to the point where you are going to do, say, a right turn, just steady the pony slightly, bringing him more into hand.

This warns the horse of a change of plan, and also gets the rider ready to apply the next aids. Just before you turn, relax the left rein so that the horse will begin to bend his head slightly to the right (lateral flexion). Then, look towards a mark on the new line of direction and drive the pony on to the right rein; this combined with a shifting of weight to the right will cause him to turn smoothly. Your left leg—which you will find is drawn back behind the girth to do it—will keep the hindquarters in the track of the forelegs; the right leg will support the pony on the circle. An additional aid is a slight movement of the hands to the right, bringing the left rein into play indirectly.

With a young animal you will use the rein more openly, that is you will move your hand out more widely to right or left, so as to lead the horse into the circle; but on no account pull the rein backwards—always *towards* the required direction. If you are going to change direction again, very soon after the first change, as in a figure of eight or serpentine, always get your horse moving in a straight line before you ask for the next turn.

If the horse hesitates, or tries to bend his head in the opposite

Plate 1

RIDING ON THE LUNGE—I

(a) *The instructor tries the lunge horse for its suitability for these lessons, while the pupil looks on*

(b) *The pupil on the move for the first time. Back is rounded and legs cling too tightly. While not nervous, she is not secure in the saddle*

(c) *Made to sit up, the pupil's body and leg positions have improved. Hands in riding position*

Plate 2

RIDING ON
THE LUNGE—2

This page shows work done by a child pupil (eleven years). The pony is an old favourite, very fat but very steady. The complete confidence between rider and mount contributed much to the success of the lessons

(a) *Mounted for the first time. Complete relaxation*

(b) *Fingers of the right hand on the pommel. Too much gripping has forced the legs back; the body is slouching with a slack waist*

(c) *Hands in the riding position. The command to sit up and straighten the back has produced a very reasonable position, seat in the correct part of the saddle*

Plate 3

RIDING ON
THE LUNGE—3

(a) *Hips firm at the trot. Rider is going confidently and easily with the pony, but slipping inwards to counteract the outward pull of the left leg. Elbows out of plane with the body stiffen the back*

(b) *Arms folded behind the back. The position is well maintained here, body well down in the saddle. Considering that this is a very fat pony, the knee and leg positions are excellent. Heel—toe—ankle combination is supple and not exaggerated*

(c) *Arms swinging upwards. Legs and lower part of the body have to act to resist the upward pull of the arms. The inside (right) leg is a little longer than the outside one. Head and neck positions are good*

Plate 4
RIDING ON THE LUNGE—4

(a) *Head turning. An advanced exercise which should only be done two or three times each way, first holding on to the saddle, as in the picture, and then with the hands in the rein-holding position. There is nothing to fault in this position and note the confidence of the pupil*

(b) *Both arms swinging, at the trot. The adult pupil is a little stiff, but is maintaining a good position well down in the saddle in spite of the vigorous upward reaction of the exercise. Leg position is good*

Plate 5

THE YOUNG HORSE ON THE LUNGE—I

(a) *Correct position of bit, bridle, cavesson noseband and lungeing rein. The side reins have not been attached*

(b) *An extremely clear and practical demonstration of introducing the young horse (or one being re-trained) to the first stages of work on the lunge. Note: 1. The light and even feel on the lunge. 2. The quiet way the assistant is leading the young horse. 3. The size of the circle, i.e. approximately 16 yards diameter. (This is about the minimum for a horse of 15 h.h. and over.) 4. The correct way of holding the leading-rein. 5. The trainer standing quietly with the whip in the left hand pointing towards the ground. 6. The trainer's right arm bent in such a position as to allow for a 'give-and-take' so that contact is maintained with the young horse*

Plate 6

THE YOUNG HORSE ON THE LUNGE—2

(a) *The assistant leads the pony into the centre, preparatory to taking over the lunge rein from the trainer, who will place himself as in the pictures below*

(b) *The trainer is roughly midway between the assistant and the young horse on the lunge. From here he can control every move of the pupil, anticipate and deal with any disobedience*

(c) *Relative positions of assistant (holding the lunge), trainer and pupil. The latter has got excited and broken into a canter, but note the complete absence of fuss on the part of the humans, so the pupil soon steadied down*

Plate 7

RIDING POSITION

(a) *A good example of the position described on page 44. The only criticism is the extreme toe position in the stirrup iron, which is apt to cause stiffness of ankle. The correct fitting of a double bridle may also be noted in this picture*

(b) *The correct — and* humane *— fitting of the dropped noseband. Note the position of the front band and its width. The thin, string-like bits of leather used by modern riders are nothing but instruments of torture*

(c) *A close-up of good toe — heel — ankle — knee combination. Note also the modern type of saddle, with knee rolls and deep seat*

Plate 8

TRANSITION—WALK TO TROT

(a)

(b)

The two pictures above show the difference between a slack and controlled transition from walk to trot

(a) *A common fault is to 'let the reins go' when applying the leg aids, resulting in loss of contact and the pony going forward at too fast a pace*

(b) *Here the aids have been applied without loss of contact, so the same pony is making the walk-trot transition quietly and smoothly*

Plate 9
TRANSITION—TROT TO CANTER

(a)

(b)

(a) *There was a jerky transition here; the pony was allowed to go forward too fast and the hands worked overtime to correct him. The right hand and the pony's head have gone up and the elbow angle is very stiff; meanwhile the left hand has gone low and forward; so the pony is in a bit of a muddle and looks it. Note the exaggerated leg aids and crouching position*

(b) *A good transition. This time hands and legs have combined correctly, with the result that the pony is leading quietly with the off fore, with an excellent head carriage. Rein contact is light but firm, hands, forearm and elbow supple. Body position is fair, and very consistent, but the rider should be looking ahead. Toes are still pointing downwards, but not so bad as in the top picture*

Plate 10

CHANGING DIRECTION

Two examples of the exercise 'from the wall to the wall'
or 'from the track to the track'

(a) *A club ride performs this exercise. Note the poles placed
to act as guides. Riders are doing the rising trot (posting)*

(b) *A young rider at the start of the exercise. The rider's
position is fair, but she has lowered her inside leg, so is not
sitting square, as she ought to be for this very slight curve. The
instructor is watching the pony's strides, to make sure that the
rhythm of the trot gait has not been altered by the change
of direction*

Plate 11

RIDING THE CANTER

Miss Sheila Willcox (now Mrs. John Waddington) and Airs and Graces (a) and High and Mighty (b). These two pictures show two different angles of the ordinary school canter:

THE HORSE. (a) *The beginning of a new stride, after the period of suspension; now the off hind has just come to the ground, and the stride will be completed with the near fore leading. Note the steadiness and perfect balance of the horse and the pleasant head carriage.* (b) *The next stage in the canter stride from the one above when both feet on the same side are on the ground; in this case the off fore is leading*

(a)

THE RIDER. *She is riding the canter smoothly without awkward bumping up and down, because her position is deep and balanced, independent of the reins and entirely at one with the movement of the horse. Note the suppleness of the body, without slackness or floppiness, upright and square to the front; straight line from elbow, via hands and reins, to the bit. It may be noted that with the less advanced horse* (a) *the ball of the foot is resting on the stirrup iron, while with High and Mighty there is toe contact only; leg aids are applied without unnecessary movement. Rein contact is firm but light. High and Mighty has his mouth closed but has lightly flexed his lower jaw. Airs and Graces shows greater flexion, perhaps a shade too much, but contact is soft*

(b)

Plate 12

JUMPING—I

(a) *First stage. The wrong way. Whether horse or rider is the pupil, the former must be presented at the obstacle under proper control*

(b) *Correct. The horse, correctly presented, is going over smoothly, picking its feet up well, having a good look at the obstacle*

(a) *This horse has reached the stage of going over a series of* cavalletti *at the trot. The free cadenced movement and good head carriage may be compared with the horse in Plate 12. The rider is sitting well, with pleasant contact, looking ahead*

Plate 13

JUMPING—2

) *A further stage of this exercise is to follow the series with a small mp, as here. Rider's position is good, though the back is a little stiff. The rse is jumping freely but with signs of excitement, steadied, however, by the preliminary trot over the* cavalletti *(above)*

(a) *Here are examples of trot approach and leap at a more advanced—but still elementary—stage of the jumping course. The horse is going forward at a good trot, seen here about 10 yards from the jump. The rider's excellent position should be noted, with stirrup leathers shortened by two holes for jumping*

Plate 14

JUMPING—3

(b) *A simple 3-foot post and rails, well taken, with a good rounded curve of the body. The rider has given the head complete freedom, to the extent of losing contact momentarily—a fault on the right side in the case of a young horse. Note the comfortably fitted noseband and absence of martingale*

Plate 15

JUMPING — 4

(a) *Intermediate—parallel bars (2 ft. 6 in. high, 3 ft. apart). The horse has jumped freely, with a flattish trajectory, adapted to the obstacle. Rider is well balanced, knee and calf firm against the saddle, ankle and foot supple and well positioned, giving full extension to the head and neck, with light and accurate contact*

(b) *Real jumping—triple bar (maximum height 4 ft. 1 in., spread 5 ft.). The horse has a perfect* bascule, *back arched, head and neck fully extended, with the greatest possible activity. The rider was a shade behind the movement, compensated for by the reaching forward of the hands and arms*

The take-off

The take-off the most important part of a jump so we present a analysis of tw different method of approach

Elevated impulsion

(a) *Miss Pa Smythe. The hors has been ridde into the jump wit* an extremely collected gait, the forehand 'lightened' by each successive step prior the actual take-off. At this moment the centre of gravity has been placed below an in a vertical line with the lowest part of the seat of the saddle. The propulsion thoroughly harmonized with the elevated thrust and is mechanically sound, for succe. the harmony between horse and rider shown here is essential*

Forward propulsion

(b) *In this photograph the rider has taken the full advantage of balanced forwar riding. The horse has been allowed to check and control its own position once the rider was satisfied that a balanced approach had been made into the jumping zone. In this way very little abnormal effort is required from the horse, and the greatest benefit is achieved by the use of locomotion as a secondary aid to minimize muscular effort. Of the two styles this one is the less wearing both for horse and rider* (b)

Plate 17

JUMPING—6

The Italian, Caprilli, evolved the classical show jumping style some fifty years ago, and two outstanding modern examples of it are Italians—the D'Inzeo brothers, Piero and Raimundo. This picture shows Captain Piero D'Inzeo and Uruguay, displaying the classic jumping position to perfection. Note the flowing line elbow—wrist—hand—reins—mouth; the contact is firm, the forward movement of the hands having given the necessary freedom to the horse's head and neck. The angle of thigh—knee—calf to foot is perfect. The body is well balanced and going with the movement, having a wonderful fluidity and suppleness that is characteristic of the rider. Note the plain noseband (made even milder by the sheepskin) and no martingale

Plate 18

JUMPING—7

Another example of the classic show jumping position of a modern rider, Hugh Wiley (U.S.A.) and Master William, winners of the King George V Cup at the Royal International Horse Show 1958. Here we have well-drilled correctness in every detail. Note the firm position of knee and calf, toes perhaps pointed out too much; the good forearm—hand—and rein position, though there is some stiffness of the wrist. The horse is well extended, having jumped with great freedom. The dropped noseband is correctly fitted, but the front strap could be broader. The running martingale does not restrict him in any way. The whole effect is pleasing

Plate 19

MANE-PLAITING

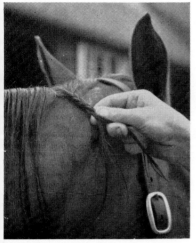

(a) *Having brushed the mane down smoothly with a damp brush, take the first lock—about width of a normal horse comb—and plait in three strands*

(b) *Sew up the end of the plait*

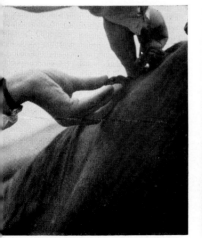

(c) *Turn the end underneath and roll it up tightly and sew up close to the crest of the neck. This picture shows the first plait completed and the second being rolled up*

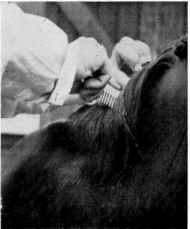

(d) *Separate the next lock with the comb and proceed as before. Normally there should be seven plaits. Finally the forelock is treated in the same way*

Plate 20

GROOMING

(a) *Essential grooming kit,* left to right, top row: *dandy brush (tail and mane), sweat scraper, curry-comb (metal), body brush.* Bottom row: *water brush, sponges (one for dock and sheath, one for eyes and nose), hoof pick, wisp, comb, all on a stable rubber. A most useful extra is a rubber curry-comb for thick and muddy coats*

(b) *Brushing. Stand away, use a nearly straight arm using weight of the body, long sweeping strokes with the lie of the hair, running the brush through the curry-comb (in right hand) after each stroke to remove dust. At intervals knock the dust out of the curry-comb where it cannot be blown away. Reverse the position on the other side of the horse. After the brush-work, go over the horse with handrubbing, using full weight of body on hands and forearms, in a circular motion. Time 30 to 45 minutes*

(c) *Finally, sponge out dock and sheath, face, eyes, nostrils. Then clean out the feet. Picture shows correct method of holding up the hind foot; pulled out towards the rear and held in place by knee and thigh of the groom*

direction, use your legs as described above, only more strongly, holding the hands still, so as to drive him forward on to the bit. Do not start pulling his head about.

Turning at the Halt

Turn on the quarters. The turn on the quarters is usually carried out at the halt, but can also be done from the move. Here is the official definition:

> The horse's forehand is moved in even, quiet and regular steps round the horse's inner hindleg. The inner hindleg, acting as a pivot, should remain as nearly as possible on the same spot. . . . When done from the walk the movement is executed in the same manner as above, but without any definite halt; the horse is taken fluently from the walk into the turn on the haunches.
>
> When done from the trot, the pace must be reduced to a walk, the horse taken instantly and fluently into a turn on the haunches and the trot resumed immediately on the completion of the turn.
>
> (Notes on Dressage—Supplementary Training Movements.)

There is a slight difference here from the pirouette, and it is worth quoting what the F.E.I. Rules say about it.

> *Half-pirouette*. This is the half-turn on the haunches. The forehand commences the half-turn, tracing a half circle round the haunches, without pausing, at the moment the inside hindleg ceases its forward movement. The horse moves forward again, without a pause, upon completion of the half-turn.
>
> During this movement the horse should maintain his impulsion and should never in the slightest move backwards or deviate sideways. It is customary that the inside hindleg while forming the pivot should return to the same spot each time it leaves the ground.
>
> (Chapter IV, Article 3. General Instructions for Dressage, 187.)

When the turn on the quarters is done at the halt in a test, you have to make a definite halt, pause, then make the turn—usually a half-turn of 180 degrees—before moving on. The turn should be a rhythmical movement with a light but definite beat of the footfalls as it progresses step by step. The inside hindleg is the pivot of the movement and should remain as nearly rooted to the ground as possible. There should be no backward movement of any kind during the turn.

To accomplish this exercise gracefully the horse must be light on the hand and on his hocks. A horse or pony that is heavy in front or leans on the bit will always have difficulty in making a really light and attractive turn. The secret of lightness is the proper use of the legs and back muscles of the rider.

When learning the movement or teaching it to your pony, do not attempt more than a quarter turn (90 degrees), and divide that into three steps of 30 degrees each. First of all, come to a good halt position along the side of the school or manège, the horse light and united, weight squarely on all four feet. (Let us assume that it is a turn to the right.) With the right rein, invite the pony to move towards the right. The legs must stimulate movement, which, restrained by the unyielding hands, will not be forward but must follow the direction of the right rein aid. The legs must also restrain the hindquarters from swinging out to the left, and the weight of the body immobilizes the inside hindleg and foot. The left rein will remain in contact in support of the movement. As soon as the pony has taken one step, pause and express approval. Do not, however, change your position or let him relax. Then give the aids smoothly for the next step, and pause again, as before, without relaxing or changing positions: the right hindfoot should still be on the ground and pointing towards the original direction.

With a young or awkward horse two steps will probably be more than enough for the first lesson. Let the pony move forward from his new position, and take him round the school for a change before having another try. Don't hurry the pony; and don't worry if it takes several days to get the third step.

At the third step, the right hindfoot will be almost completely twisted, and you should make a definite halt here to allow him to adjust both his feet to the new direction. Then, as before, move forward in the new direction; on no account let the pony step backwards.

Once these first three steps have been correctly mastered, you will have no difficulty about the half- or even full- turn. If the pony has done the half-turn correctly, you should find that he is now standing just off the original track. In a test you will of course put him back on to the track in the course of two or three steps after moving off.

Turn on the forehand. To turn on the forehand, adopt the same procedure as above, except that this time your weight is slightly forward, your hands restrain forward movement, and your legs stimulate the movement of the quarters round the forehand.

Most horses learn this movement only too easily. It is a useful exercise for making the horse obedient to lateral aids, that is leg and rein aids on the same side of the horse; also as a refresher for horses which have become insensitive to leg aids. It is a good exercise, too, in aid application for beginner riders, and is of course of practical value in the fields when opening gates; but it should be used sparingly at all times. It is not a school figure.

Balance, Flexion, Collection

The untrained horse is seldom correctly balanced for riding, that is with his weight at the halt evenly distributed between all four legs, instead of a natural tendency to be overweighted on the forehand, which is the heaviest part of the horse. The rider's position in the saddle, unless other forces are brought into play to adjust the balance, i.e. engagement of the quarters and lightening of the forehand will enhance that tendency.

At the halt, the F.E.I. definition goes on to say, the horse 'should be ready to move off at the slightest indication of the rider. The neck raised, the poll high, the head a little in front of the vertical, the mouth light, the horse champing his bit and maintaining a light contact with the rider's hand.'

These desirable objects are gained in the first place by *flexion*, which is the flexing or giving of the lower jaw of the horse and a bending-in of his head from the poll, his neck remaining in exactly the same position. Flexion obtained by the bending of the neck results in a lowering of the head and in the horse becoming over-bent and behind the bit, which means that the mouth and jaw have lost contact with the bit.

The beginning of flexion can come with work on the lunge, when the horse first begins to learn to carry his head correctly and to get the feel of the bit and chew it. If the side reins have been correctly fitted, he should automatically begin to flex his jaw as the forward movement pushes him up to the bit, without being over-restrained and so feeling the need to escape from the bit.

If all has gone well on the lunge, flexion should come quietly and naturally when ridden work begins. The rider cautiously maintains light contact with the mouth and by a series of gentle vibrations—a finger action—invites the horse to relax his jaw, *without* bending his head in any other way. It is a question of 'feeling' as is all successful horsemanship; the rider should know through the reins

67

when the jaw has relaxed; there will be slight lessening of tension and the horse should champ lightly at the bit. This stage can be done quite well in a snaffle. The rider maintains forward impulsion with his legs, this being the foundation of correct flexion.

The whole process is a subtle relation between horse and rider, requiring the exercise of 'equestrian tact', which is mainly the knowledge of when to stop asking the horse to do something before he decides on his own that he has had enough of it.

The development of flexion and the bending of the head from the poll are achieved concurrently with the rest of the training of the horse, in due course with the double bridle and curb bit.

Specific flexing exercises should be carried out first at the halt then at the walk. Once flexion is achieved at those paces it can be obtained at all times. It can also be lost by a weak rider who relies on the reins and horse's mouth to keep his balance.

Lateral flexion is when the horse is asked to bend his head to right or left for changes of direction and work on two tracks, which are explained later.

Successful flexion depends to some extent on the conformation of the horse's head and neck. Horses, especially ponies, with thick necks and closely coupled jaws will never be able to flex properly or happily beyond a certain stage. If the jaws are set too close together, they will press against the neck when attempting to bend the head from the poll, causing pain and discomfort which will produce the inevitable resistance and stiffening.

The rider or trainer should study the conformation of a horse's head and neck very carefully, for in many ways it is the key to successful control and certainly to any advanced or fast work. A horse required to play polo, for example, will never be any real good if it has not complete freedom of movement of the head and neck; any attempt to pull it up sharply, which is the essence of polo, will cause pain and end in a hard mouth and stiff jaw.

The main reason why children have so much difficulty with their ponies is because of the bad conformation of so many of their necks, especially of coarse-bred ones. The answer is to realize the limitations and not to expect too much.

Only the minimum bend should be required, obtained more by a yielding of the opposite rein rather than by extra tension on the direct rein, and by the action of the legs, impelling and supporting.

With a young horse it may be necessary to use the direct rein more obviously the first two or three lessons to the right or left, in order to give it a clear idea of what is required. The great thing to be avoided is a bending of the middle part of the neck, which will lead to evasions, being over-bent, and faulty action.

Correct flexion is the basis of *collection*, which is a portmanteau word covering a whole range of effects. In French and German, especially, there are several words to describe different degrees of collection, e.g. *Mise en main, raccourci, ramener, rassembler*.

In its basic form 'collection' is the uniting of the horse by the action of the leg and the restraint of a light but steady hand to induce the horse to stand at attention with hindquarters under him, not left behind, so that the forehand is lightened and the centre of gravity—at the halt—coinciding more or less with the rider's position in the lowest point of the saddle.

In this degree of collection the horse's head should be carried naturally, about 30 degrees off the vertical, muzzle about level with the rider's knees.

It is in fact hardly collection at all, but the preliminary to it, better called 'uniting' the horse, or first engagement of the hindquarters. In the first lessons of forward movement and balancing exercises this is all that is required.

The beginnings of flexion and collection can be obtained with a snaffle bit, but the trainer must be content with very little of either and not ask for too much. Too much action on the snaffle will either raise the head too much and produce a poking nose or force it downwards and backwards into the chest. In either case a dead mouth will be the end product.

This is where equestrian tact comes in, which is impossible without a firm seat, independent of the reins—a requirement which is harped on without apology throughout this book.

Collected gaits are not so much slower as shorter than ordinary ones. The action is more elevated, the strides shorter and more active. A perfectly collected movement is one that is brilliant and brimful of impulsion, the neck arched, head raised and nearly vertical, light in the forehand with croup low and the hindquarters engaged under the horse—not left behind—the hocks active, giving a high action with no dragging of the hind toes. The impression given to the spectator—and the feel to the rider—should be one of controlled power. The horse is in fact perfectly united between hand and leg.

The theory that no collection is needed for elementary work, outdoor riding, crossing country and jumping, seems to me to fall to the ground on the primacy of the rider's legs among the aids. All impulsion comes from the rear and the effect of leg action is to stimulate the natural forces of the horse. A condition of forward

69

movement and also balance is a lightening of the forehand through the steadying action of the independent hands on the reins, which unites the front and back ends of the horse—perhaps a better name for this early stage than collection.

The problem facing trainer and rider at all times is to decide what degree of unity or collection is sufficient for the stage reached or the objects in view; to avoid the danger of over-collection. The problem is an individual one peculiar to each horse; only experience can help to solve it.

Over-collection can be avoided by being very sparing with collected exercises in the early stages, following them with spells of complete relaxation, with free rein work. If the horse becomes over-bent, the best remedy is to free his head and neck completely; work on the lunge, perhaps; free jumping in a lane to encourage him to extend himself; change from a curb bit back to a snaffle.

The change from snaffle to double bridle will depend on individual circumstances, but generally the latter can be introduced after the balancing exercises and before lateral work begins.

It is best to hold the snaffle reins in one hand and the curb reins in the other. The former will keep the head in position, while action of legs and curb reins will encourage the relaxing of the lower jaw and the bending of the head from the poll. Rein contact should be of the very lightest, a continual taking and giving through a vibration of the fingers in a steady hand. Anything like sustained resistance by the hands or a steady pull must be avoided.

The trainer should have sensitive fingers and supple wrists, so that he will feel the slightest giving of the jaw and be enabled to give immediately in his turn, thus acquiring a subtle sympathetic contact between himself and his horse.

The degree of collection which can be obtained in any horse will depend entirely on its conformation, character and the potentialities of its intelligence—and this applies more definitely to ponies, as I have mentioned above. The wise trainer will recognize the limits of his pupil's powers and not attempt to go beyond them by force. At all times he will do well to remember those words of Xenophon, written two and a quarter millenia ago—and even then quoting a yet earlier authority, Simon of Athens:

'. . . what a horse does under compulsion he does blindly and his performance is no more beautiful than would be that of a ballet dancer taught by whip and goad . . . what we need is that the horse should of his own accord exhibit his finest airs and graces at set signals.'

Lateral Movement

When (a) the rider's position is well stabilized at all paces in a straight line and on a circle, and the leg aids can be applied independently, and (b) the horse or pony is able to go perfectly on a straight line and is nicely in hand and supple, lateral work can begin.

There are two kinds of lateral movements:

(i) With the bend of the head opposite to the direction of movement.

(ii) With the bend towards the direction of movement.

(i) This is a training exercise in the school known as 'shoulder-in'. This movement was initiated by a great French equestrian, François de la Guérinière (c. 1690–1751). He regarded it as 'the first and last of all the lessons we can give the horse in order to obtain complete suppleness and perfect freedom in all parts of his body. . . .', and it has remained one of the best exercises in all equitation schools ever since. It is sufficient to quote the latest modern writer on the subject:

'The object of this movement is to increase the lightness and suppleness of the horse, and to obtain a higher degree of obedience. These exercises improve the activity of the hind legs, and the horse becomes more responsive to the rider's leg and rein aids.'

Richard L. Wätchen, *Dressage Riding*.
(English translation 1958.)

The shoulder-in movement is that in which the horse moves in a diagonal position without changing the original direction of movement. The quarters follow the original track close to the side of the school, while the head, neck and shoulders are bent inwards towards the inside of the school, the legs moving in a separate track parallel to the original one. The head, neck, and shoulders are bent inwards (i.e. towards the inside of the school) round the rider's inside leg, and the horse is flexed in opposition to the direction of movement.

A good way to initiate this movement is to start it at one corner of the school, carrying on the circle so that the horse is at an angle to the side, and then checking him with the outside rein and using the inside leg to make him move sideways parallel to the side of the school. The inside rein will continue to lead the forehand round, so that the horse is bent against the direction of move-

71

ment. To recapitulate briefly: the inside rein leads the horse into the diagonal position, while the outside rein checks it and holds it in the required angle; the inside leg gives the impulse to continue the movement sideways, while the outside leg holds the quarters in position. The rider's body should remain upright with a bracing of the back, and with a slight lengthening of the inside leg.

In the shoulder-out the horse's quarters are on the inside track, and the forward legs are on the outside track, in other words the reverse of shoulder-in. Once again, the head, neck, and shoulders are flexed round the outside leg of the rider, and the bend is in the opposite direction of movement.

Other variations of this exercise are:

Quarters-in (*travers*), in which the horse's forelegs remain in the original track, while the quarters move in a parallel track inside, but the head, neck, and shoulders are bent round the rider's inside leg and in the direction of movement.

Quarters-out (*renvers*), in which the above movement is reversed.

The angle of the horse's body to the wall in all these movements is usually not more than 30 degrees.

(ii) *Half-pass*. In this exercise the horse moves away from the original track at the side of the school at an angle of about 45 degrees diagonally across the school, its forelegs and hindlegs moving in two tracks one behind the other across the school. The horse's body should be as nearly parallel to the side of the school as possible, with the head and neck bent slightly in the direction of movement. The horse's outside leg should cross in front of the inside leg, both fore and hind.

As we have seen, a change of direction (from the wall to the wall) can be the beginning of this movement. It can also be obtained from work on the circle, which if correctly done, prepares the horse's muscles for this work.

Rein Back

Some authorities consider that this movement should not be begun until the horse is well advanced in its training. But, as it is a most essential practical requirement of a horse at all times, there seems no reason why he should not be introduced quietly to the movement from time to time before serious training begins. After all, even the youngest colt is frequently asked to rein back a step or two when being shown off, or photographed, or in the stable. A step back, every now and then after a rest period when lungeing, can get the pupil used to the movement.

Serious training should not normally begin until the horse is established in forward movement at the trot and accepts the bit calmly.

Preliminary lessons can begin on the ground; they should be done along the side of the school, or wall or hedge, so that the horse can be kept straight. Stand in front of the horse, holding the reins in the left hand, behind the jaw; lungeing whip is on the right hand to act as the leg aid and to keep the pupil's quarters from swinging out away from the wall.

Gently encourage the horse to lower its head slightly and to flex its jaw, at the same time touching his flank with the whip. Once he has taken one step, stop and make much of him. The great thing is to achieve the amount of movement you require and no more. Above all do not let the horse lose contact with the bit by moving his whole head back and away from it—getting what is called behind the bit —when he will be out of control.

After one step—which is back with one diagonal, say near hind and off fore—pause, then try to get the next step with the other diagonal to complete one stride. Halt for another reward, while he calms down after that exciting exercise and stands steady. Then lead him forward a few strides, halt and repeat the lesson. This done three times will be quite enough for the first lesson.

This exercise helps to increase the agility of the horse, to strengthen and supple the back with his head raised. The advantage of starting on the ground is that you can place his head in a convenient low position. This lightens the hindquarters, enabling them to move back calmly. Any tendency to rush backwards should be restrained at once. The object to be attained is a long, slow stride, by diagonals—off hind, near fore; near hind, off fore—in two-time, not a four-time, sequence.

If the horse or pony—it is usually the latter—is reluctant to move, tap his coronet with your foot until he picks it up. If there is still reluctance, take the reins in each hand and vibrate them alternately.

Once you have achieved one straight backward stride, you can ask for another one in the same way. The maximum on foot should be three strides, after which the work can be carried on mounted.

When mounted lower the hands without yielding and apply the legs, so that a forward impulsion is created which, however, recoils as it were off the bit. Then a slight backward vibration of the reins combined, in early lessons, with easing forward of the body weight to release the hindquarters, will make the horse carry on the movement backwards instead of forwards. Then do not move legs or body, sit upright, and let the horse step back a pace. Then immediately relax the reins and make much of him. So step by step a quiet, rhythmical movement will be achieved. Once the impulse has been created the function of the legs is to keep the horse straight.

The Flying Change

Everyone wants to achieve the 'flying change' of leading leg at the canter. It is a delightfully rhythmic movement, full, when well done, of grace and elegance. It is worth a lot of patience to do it properly.

The nature of the act of changing the leading leg varies with the use of your horse or pony.

First, the polo pony—and this includes the gymkhana pony. The polo pony must learn to change legs on his own initiative at high speed, without any loss of that speed or of balance, without any instructions or assistance from his rider. He, with his legs and reins, swings the pony in this direction and that, and if the latter could not change its legs fluently and easily, it would cross them and come down. Nothing, I think, is smoother than a polo pony's flying change. The rider never notices it; indeed he takes it all for granted. The same applies to the gymkhana pony.

Second, the show horse or pony. You do not need the niceties of dressage for him. A shifting of the weight with a change of direction, to throw him off his balance, will make him change. You are not going at the speed of polo, nor is the change of direction so sharp and sudden, so he has plenty of time to recover his balance by swapping to the inside leg in the lead.

Third is the trained horse, whom you want to change on a straight line precisely at your command, not before or after.

When you can make your pony strike off quietly and smoothly with whichever leading leg you ask for you can start on the canter change.

As always, begin at the beginning—in a circle, say on the right rein, canter, right leg leading, quietly on a large circle—half the school—a few times, then as you come to the centre of the school, drop down softly to a trot and then walk; pass the centre and begin to make a left circle at the trot in the other half of the school. After a few more trot strides—never mind how many at first—obtain a canter with the left leg leading. Circle to the left a few times, then make the same change back again, and so on, gradually reducing the number of trot strides each time until you can eliminate this altogether and do the change in three or four walk strides.

Then go through the same sequence on the diagonals across the school until you have once again made the sequence canter—walk—

canter. Never mind how long this takes so long as every transition is done correctly and softly.

Once you are sure of yourself and of the aids, and find that the pony understands them, you can start reducing the walk steps, until one day, quite naturally, you will give the correct aid for the new leading leg just before the pony gets into the suspension phase of his canter on the original leading leg, and you will have accomplished the flying change.

Further Progress

The work done so far should have laid the foundation for further progress to the higher levels of equitation, which entirely depends on the potentialities of horse or rider. This only a competent instructor or trainer can decide.

There are no new aids for obtaining advanced high school movements; all the principles given so far hold good and it is a question now of the individual relations between horse and rider, increasing sensitiveness to the 'feels' of riding, more subtle indications and reactions to them.

The basis of all advanced work is collection and the fullest engagement of the hindquarters under the horse with a corresponding lightening of the forehand—strong leg and light hand. At this stage the collected horse should carry his head almost vertical, with easy flexion of jaw and head from the poll, without too much shortening of the neck.

Collected movements now should be high and brilliant, not a long step from the piaffe and the passage.

The opposite of collection is extension, and the correct transitions from one pace to another is an essential part of the advanced training.

Like collection, extension covers a wide range of performance. At the beginning it is nothing more than fast trot with rather longer strides than normal. The essence of good extension is that correct cadence and rhythm must be maintained, and that the extension of stride must come from the impulsion of the hindquarters.

While moderate collection and extension are part of basic equitation and work in the open, maximum collection (*rassembler*) and extension are advanced school and competition movements and the basis of high school.

Extension should only be begun when the ordinary gaits of the horse—walk, trot, and canter—have been firmly and correctly established, that is to say performed with a steady, regular rhythm and cadence, with no unevenness.

Then, using the long side of the school or the diagonal across the school, gradually increase the leg action while *holding* the contact with the horse's mouth. There must be no pulling, the hands steady and not yielding. Hands should be held lower than normal, supporting a lower carriage of the horse's head and neck in proportion to the extension of the stride. Everything starts from the leg action which stimulates a more active and longer hock action, which in its turn produces greater activity of the shoulders and a lengthening of the foreleg stride.

The rider should be able to feel this increased activity beneath him and should not ask for too much extension at first or for too long—two strides correctly done are ample.

After doing this a couple of times, relax quietly into an ordinary gait, do a little free rein work; then start again. Do not ask for extension more than half a dozen times or so in an ordinary school lesson. After about a week or ten days you can ask for three or four strides, and eventually, in another fortnight or three weeks, depending on progress, you can obtain six steps.

From this point the obtaining of maximum extension depends on the potentialities of horse and rider. Not every horse is going to qualify for Grand Prix dressage or anywhere near it; but steady preparation and sympathetic work will take the dullest pupil a long way further than might at first appear possible. It is part of equestrian tact to know the limitations of the horse and not to press him unduly beyond them.

None of this work can be successfully accomplished without an instructor on the ground who knows what he is doing, can see the correct movements and instantly check faults.

Turns and Pirouettes

At this stage it should be possible to practise complete turns on the haunches at the halt (page 65) as a preliminary to turns on the move—pirouettes.

The *pirouette* is described by the F.E.I. as

'a small circle on two tracks, with a radius equal to the length of the horse, the forehand moving round the haunches.

At whatever pace the pirouette is executed, the horse should turn smoothly, maintaining the exact cadence and sequence of legs at that pace.'

As in the turn at the halt, the horse pivots on the inside leg, which is, however, raised and lowered in time with the rhythm of the movement, as near to the same spot as possible. The number of strides taken to accomplish this movement is about five.

This is an advanced high school movement, its success depending on the perfection of collection attained. It can be practised in the preliminary work already described; the exercise of reducing the circle also makes a good preparation for it. Absolute precision is not essential here, provided that the correct cadence of the gait is maintained.

It is also part of the training for polo or gymkhanas, not to mention speed competitions in show jumping. Here quickness rather than precision is required, combined with lightness of hand, for which correct basic training is essential.

In this case a horse or pony should learn to become bridlewise, that is to respond to the leg aids only with the lightest indications from the reins on the neck. This is just as much an art as any other form of equitation, represented in its highest form by the American cutting horse, which cuts out and segregates an unruly calf from a herd without a bit in its mouth at all; yet it preserves perfect balance and a surprising degree of collection. Too much concentration on competition dressage and 'contact' has tended towards the neglect of riding 'bridlewise'.

The best way to obtain the 'school' pirouette is from the *renvers* exercise (page 72). Begin at the walk, which must be fully collected, and come into the *renvers* position a full stride from the side of the school so that there is plenty of room for the turn. Proceed to the corner and continue the bend so that it merges into a turn on the haunches on the move. The legs maintain impulsion, the outside leg and the inside rein guiding the horse round in the correct bend, and both reins restraining forward movement.

A three-quarter turn brings the horse again into a *renvers* position in the direction of the next corner of the school where the movement can be repeated. Once the rhythm of the exercise has been established, the full turn can be attempted from the straight in the centre of the school. The same process can then be repeated at the canter. Before moving into the *renvers* position the correct cadence of a fully collected canter should be firmly established.

Never attempt these exercises at the beginning of a lesson, or if things have not gone well. Horse and rider should be mentally as well as physically prepared for every new item on the curriculum.

Controlled Flying Change

The canter and changes of lead have already been dealt with (page 74); if left to itself a horse will do flying changes with the greatest of ease and fluency. The difference between that and high school work is that the horse must change his leading leg at the canter at the will of the rider; equally, not change it at all, as in the counter-canter.

The school flying change requires maximum impulsion, performed of course always at a collected canter, the drive coming from the hindquarters with the forehand as light as possible, and no deviation from the straight line of movement. Therefore the rider should be as still as possible in the saddle, using his back and legs to produce the impulsion and avoiding any shifting of weight to one side or the other.

The first stage is to get the horse to change at the exact spot fixed by the rider. All this work should be done on the diagonals in the centre of the school—or in the open for that matter, but away from the sides of the school. Start with a mark—a whitewashed peg —in the centre of the school and obtain the change exactly at that spot. Immediately, then, vary the position of the peg all along the line of movement, so that the horse is prepared to change at any moment and does not get into the habit of anticipating the aids.

Once this is done, use two markers, one at the beginning of the diagonal and one towards the other end. If you come to the corner at a counter-canter, this is all part of the discipline of the lesson.

The next stage is to introduce the change at a given number of strides after the first stage. Begin with about eight and gradually reduce to four. From there you can progress from two to three and four changes. Then gradually reduce the interval to two strides, and aim at achieving as near perfection as possible, before embarking on the change at every stride.

Always allow enough distance on the diagonal before the first change in order to give the horse time to settle down and gain the necessary impulsion. The rider must be completely with the movement, and the aids should be applied punctually and quickly.

Piaffe and Passage

The *piaffe* is a highly collected trot without forward movement— marking time, in fact. The *passage* should be obtained from the *piaffe*, and is that measured highly cadenced elevated trot which is so spectacular when properly done, with the pointing of the toes and the slight hesitation before each footfall.

These two movements are essentially high school ones, gymnastic exercises which are the foundation of the 'airs' of the classical school—*levade, courbette, capriole*, etc. This is not a 'high school' book, so I shall not attempt to describe the training for them in detail.

In the Spanish Riding School the horse comes to the *piaffe* after his first two years of basic training, and is taught on the ground with reins held short. As usual the process is gradual and a little forward movement is allowed at first; then follows work between the pillars (the invention of the French riding master de Pluvinel [*c.* 1623]), and finally under saddle. The *passage* is obtained *through* the *piaffe*, and that is always the correct sequence of training.

The good *piaffe* should be executed lightly, the hindquarters very well engaged and active. The feet should be raised in the diagonal rhythm of the trot, high and definite, the hind feet almost as high as the forefeet. The body should be quite straight without any rolling or swinging of the quarters.

The qualities of the *passage* are the same, only the horse moves forward at a high, elevated and graceful gait, gaining very little ground at each step.

5

Jumping

How a Horse Jumps

Ponies and horses are said not to jump naturally, in distinction from the dog or the cat—or the deer family for that matter. This is open to question, for the lives and purposes of all these creatures are quite different. The cat and dog tribe tend to be pouncing and bounding animals, short in the neck and light in weight in proportion to their muscles, with a bone structure adapted to their mode of progression. Horses and ponies, grazing animals with long necks, do not live and move by jumping, but they *can* jump if they have to—in order to escape from danger or get to some desired place, and *their* muscles and skeletons are well adapted for these special efforts.

In nature, without human interference, the horse's natural leap is extended and arched. The jump is truly an extension of the stride of a horse, as is specially noticeable in a long flat jump over water. If the horse sees an obstacle in front of him, and is quite unimpeded—and really wants to get to the other side—he will stretch his head and neck to have a good look at it, gather his hindquarters under him, contracting the spring, and then stretch out his muscles to drive his body forwards and upwards. Then he will tuck his forelegs under him and swing up and down over the crest of the obstacle so as to make the jump with the least expenditure of energy. When he lands the weight comes on his two fore pasterns, which bend right back into the ground, and he tends to raise his head and neck as a counterbalance to the raising of the quarters to clear the fence. Then the quarters come to the ground and once more propel the front end forward, and he resumes his normal stride with usually the same leading foreleg, but he may change in order to regain lost balance.

We have all known of horses jumping out of stables and over very high fences when no one was looking. One special case, I remember, of a remount at Saugor in India: completely raw, something of a rogue, he had not even begun to be *taught* to jump; yet he escaped from his stable one night, doing a standing jump of about 5 feet 6 inches, with barely the depth of his girth to spare over the top bar. If that was not a case of a well-arched trajectory and perfect *bascule*, nothing is!

Some ponies and horses will do this better than others of course, but they will all do it quite well enough—if left alone. It is the rider's weight which upsets the balance and makes an untrained horse—physically as well as educationally—awkward and uncomfortable. This brings about stiffness and causes the all-too-frequent hollow back seen in competitions.

In the jump of the stiff or hollow-backed horse there is little movement of the spine, so the horse has to lift himself higher to get over the jump rather than flow over it, and exert far greater physical effort than the horse whose correct training has preserved his natural suppleness.

So the object of all training is, or should be, to make the horse or pony supple and keep him so. One certain cause of stiffness and creator of hollow backs in jumping is hurry. If you ask the horse or pony to do more than his muscular development will allow him to do easily, he has to make special efforts, which make him stiffen himself—rather like 'pressing' your shots at tennis or cricket or golf. This does not mean that you must spend years and years on the job, but that you must watch the general physical development of the young animal so that it prepares him for the work ahead.

To be sure, the horse or pony is such a powerful creature that he can surmount almost any obstacle *in spite* of hindrance from the rider caused by either bad training or bad riding, or both. Consequently he is for ever flattering us by giving an inflated idea of our own prowess and skill.

Equipment

Lack of space and proper equipment handicap the correct systematic training of both horse and rider, but a good deal can be done in limited space and with local materials.

It is better to use a few well-made obstacles with solid poles than to have a lot of flimsy twigs and broomsticks dotted about the place. The horse—the pony even more so—soon learns to treat them with contempt, and it is very difficult to persuade him to change his mind.

The basic requirement is poles, at least 8 feet long and 3 to 4 inches in diameter. Larch, birch or ash are the best materials

Twelve such poles will provide a sufficient variety of jumps for elementary training.

The next need is stands for the poles and other fences. The best arrangement, if the land conditions allow it, is to have more poles similar to those mentioned above in 4- and 5-foot lengths, sunk in pairs one foot deep into the ground and a minimum of 8 feet apart. These poles should have holes drilled in them at 3-inch intervals from 1 foot high to the top for the insertion of pegs or cups to take the cross poles.

Finally you need about six pairs of X-shaped trestles with a long and a short side, between which you nail and solidly fix one of your poles, so that, according to the way in which you lay the trestle, you can have an obstacle 1 foot high, 6 inches, and practically lying on the ground.

A supply of sheep hurdles is useful for wings, enclosures, backing open fences and so forth; but see that all the projecting poles on one side of each hurdle are sawn off flush with the actual hurdle part. Useful additions, which can usually be obtained fairly cheaply are oil drums and old ammunition boxes. Disused doors and planks of all kinds can also be pressed into use, strengthened by the other materials. A 10-foot length of old iron piping, 1-inch diameter, is also useful.

It cannot be emphasized too strongly that all your jumping equipment should look and be as solid and unbreakable as possible.

If possible have a lane, and a series of obstacles for a young animal to jump for his food. This is an ideal, not essential, but worth providing if conditions permit. It is a short corridor with three or four fences—or only two, or even one—through which the trainee must go for his supper or his drink. Hurdles can provide the corridor and poles, about 10 feet apart, the obstacles. It is essential that these poles should be fixed, so that they cannot be knocked down, but also removable so that you can progressively raise the height of the obstacles. If you are dealing with a complete youngster, start at 6 inches high and gradually increase to about 18 inches.

The sole purpose of this is to establish confidence in the horse, to get him to associate jumping with something pleasant, to enjoy the sensation of jumping, and to build up his muscles and make him supple.

If this kindergarten 'play-pen' training can be achieved at the outset, the subsequent work will be all the easier. It can be carried out with a horse or pony of any age, who is having jumping lessons for the first time, and contemporaneously with the formal training.

82

It can be part of the re-training process too.

With the materials listed above it is possible to reproduce almost any kind of show jump up to heights of 3 feet. You begin with the straightforward post and rails. For parallel bars, start with a pair of fixed uprights and build up a second post-and-rails behind it with the trestles (known as *cavalletti*—plural of the Italian word for trestle, *cavalletto*—because their use was invented by Captain [now General] Ubertalli of the Italian army many years ago), at whatever spread distance is required. A *cavalletto* placed in front of a post-and-rails makes the beginning of a triple bar, easily developed by the use of more *cavalletti*. The door can become the basis of a wall or other solid-looking obstacles. Hurdles interlaced with green branches and laid against the post-and-rails can imitate a brush fence.

Oil drums are best used cut in half and in a row of uprights, half-filled with earth to make them solid and not so noisy when hit; but hammer down any sharp edges. They can be laid on their sides and used in combinations with poles to make a hog's back type of jump. Several of them filled with earth and covered again with earth and turfed can become a small bank. Wooden boxes can also be used in a variety of combinations, sufficient for the heights required in the elementary training.

Jumping Training
(Illustrated, Plates 12—18)

The object of all training, of both horse and rider, should be:

1. To establish confidence in each other.
2. To achieve a fluent steady approach to the obstacle, a smooth jump with rounded back, a quick get-away on landing, with complete freedom for the head and neck of the horse and the minimum of interference or movement by the rider.

Jumping training can go side by side with ordinary schooling, all the work on the flat being both preparatory and complementary to the jumping.

For the horse, the best preparation is the work on the lunge and the balancing exercises, which should have suppled and strengthened his muscles, especially those of the neck and back, and taught him to balance himself and use his hindquarters.

For the rider, the best preparation is the riding on the lunge which will give him the independent and balanced seat and the ability to move in harmony with the horse.

Although *show* jumping is a highly specialized branch of equestrianism, *jumping* is an integral part of riding, developing naturally from the regular systematic training. It has already been included in the programme of training given on page 21.

The sequence of lessons now given can be fitted into the main syllabus without any difficulty.

1. Free jumping in lane. (As described above, this can begin at any time.)
2. Riding over single small obstacles (*cavalletti* at their lowest level or poles on the ground).
3. Riding over poles or low *cavalletti* in series of two or three at a time, at varying distances.
4. Repetition of 2 and 3 over progressively raised obstacles, 6 to 12 inches.
5. *Cavalletti* in series of three, maximum four, one stride then half a stride apart.
6. Single low *cavalletto* in combination with a higher jump (2 feet.)
7. *Cavalletti series*, as in 5, in combination with a higher jump.
8. Trotting over a variety of obstacles from 2 feet to 2 feet 6 inches.
9. As above, raising heights to 2 feet 9 inches.
10. Repetition at the canter.
11. Cross-country work at trot and canter over as many small obstacles as possible, up and down hill, etc.
12. Work in the school over higher obstacles, 3 feet to 3 feet 6 inches at walk, trot and canter.
13. Jumping set courses, maximum 3 feet 6 inches.
14. Repetition, heights increased to 4 feet occasionally.

The instructor can work progressively within this framework, varying the time required in each stage according to the pupils, equine or human.

Each pupil should, needless to say, be provided with an experienced partner. In either case, every horse should be provided with a neck-strap.

Preliminary, Cavalletti Work

Stages 2–4. Begin at a walk, and introduce the exercise into another lesson, quite casually. Do not halt the pupil or the ride so that it can watch preparations and begin to wonder what is going to happen. The poles should be in position already, or laid out while the ride is doing other work.

There should be no alteration in riding position but a shortening of the stirrups by one or two holes at this stage.

The pupil horse should not jump, but walk, then trot, quite smoothly over the obstacle. The rider's part is to maintain the correct amount of impulsion both before and after the obstacle, with light but definite contact.

The next stage is to have two or three poles, not less than 10 feet apart and not necessarily in series.

With the obstacles raised to 6 inches, the same smoothness is required, the horse to walk and trot over them but not jump or break into a canter at the sight of them. The cadence of the gait, whether walk or trot, should be preserved all through these exercises.

The rider should keep his legs close to the horse's sides, going with the movement without leaning excessively forward, enough only to allow the horse to stretch his neck to look at the obstacle. Hands should not be allowed to fall forward on to the horse's neck.

Stage 5. This is an important exercise for both horse and rider, teaching balance and exercising the back and neck muscles, and teaching the horse to move off his hocks.

Three *cavalletti* (6 inches) are placed in series 10 to 11 feet apart, according to the length of stride of the horse. The rider or trainer goes round the school once or twice at a steady cadenced trot, makes a wide circle—and the correctness of the application of aids for the circle is important for the success of the exercise—and approaches the series steadily without losing or increasing impulsion. Rein contact should be firm, so that the horse will trot smoothly over the three obstacles with only a slight heightening of the stride—and so increased brilliance of movement—but with no increase of pace or loss of cadence. He should not be allowed to jump or break into a canter.

When the exercise is correctly done at the larger distance close up the *cavalletti* to half a stride distance, approximately 5 feet, so that the horse places half the trot diagonal in between each pair of obstacles.

As before, the horse should be allowed to extend his head and neck by the requisite forward movement of the rider. The movement over the *cavalletti* should be a brilliant cadenced trot.

Stages 6, 7. Set up a post-and-rails, with a ground pole and one at 2 feet. Place a *cavalletto* (6 inches) about 5 strides away, and pass over both obstacles at the trot.

If the horse is inclined to be slovenly over the higher obstacle, place a thin iron bar or tubing above the top pole. If he hits this with his toes or his shins it will surprise him without hurting him unduly, and will teach him to respect the obstacle, which is better learnt at this stage than later on.

Gradually introduce another *cavalletto* about 24 feet or two strides from the jump.

As an advanced variation place a series of three *cavalletti*, the nearest two strides from the jump.

The rider's chief faults in these exercises are:

(*a*) To be left behind, with either a pull on the horse's mouth to regain his balance, or a slipping of the reins through the fingers to avoid jabbing the mouth.

(*b*) To go forward jerkily, almost ahead of the movement of the horse, with probably loss of contact and leaning on the horse's neck.

If he cannot correct them quickly, it means that his preliminary training has been inadequate.

Faults of the horse:

(*a*) Getting over-excited and rushing.

(*b*) Loss of balance.

(*c*) Not picking up the feet, stumbling.

The best correction is free work in a lane, combined with regular balancing exercises and plenty of school work on the flat at the trot.

(*d*) Not meeting the obstacles squarely, and 'wandering'.

Only the rider can correct this, by correct approach in the first place and correct application of hand and leg to keep the horse straight and up to his bit.

The *cavalletto* is a flexible instrument which can be used in any number of different ways to prepare the horse and rider for the advanced stages of jumping. Through intelligent and systematic *cavalletti* work both learn balance and to acquire the feels of jumping, without which there can be no true harmony. The rider learns to go with the horse and acquires the rudiments of the forward position. The horse exercises its neck, back, and thigh muscles, and becomes supple in preparation for the advanced work ahead. It becomes accustomed to a quiet cadenced approach to any obstacle.

Stages 8, 9. The lessons learned in the previous stages can now be applied to the beginnings of real jumping. As many small jumps, 2 feet high, as possible should be dotted about the field, not in any set pattern, and the pupils should be taken over them more or less at random, provided there is a straight approach of at least 5 strides. There should be no increase in trotting pace, but stronger leg action should produce more active hock action and increase impulsion. Two strides from the jump the rider should squeeze with his legs to give the necessary extra drive, while his hands act to maintain the cadence of the trot. As the horse takes off he will extend his head and neck, the rider leaning his body forward with the movement and his hands, lengthening the forearm and elbow, so as to allow the horse freedom to stretch forward. At this stage the rider's stirrup leathers can be shortened by one or two holes.

There should be no exaggerated forward movement of the body, no rounding of the back or throwing it forwards on to the horse's neck. From the knee to the foot the lower leg should be locked to the saddle, knee pressing against the knee rolls, lower legs immovable against the sides of the horse, foot firmly on the bar of the stirrup iron, heel down helping to keep it in place, toes pointing naturally to the front. The upper part of the body will pivot forward from the knees. The point of the elbow, forearm, hand, and rein should be in one line to the horse's mouth.

Apart from being left behind the chief fault of the rider is collapsing his body forward from the waist, like a shut knife. The movement is usually jerky, causing roughness of hand contact, and a pushing back of the posterior and so becoming behind the movement. Another fault is holding the hand at right angles to the line of the rein, which usually means loss of harmony with the horse. The fact that some successful riders have adopted this mannerism is no excuse for imitation. All flapping or waving of the legs should be avoided.

A common riding fault is to place the body forward before the horse takes off, which only results in unbalancing him, and getting ahead of the centre of gravity. If the forward movement is timed to coincide with the moment of take-off, the rider will be able to go with the centre of gravity of the horse all through the movement.

The practice of leaving the saddle altogether during the leap arose out of the idea that the more weight you take off the horse's back the better and higher he can jump, which is in fact fallacious. The F.E.I. world's record high jump of 8 feet 1.2 inches (by Captain A. P. Morales, of Chile, on Huaso, 1949) was achieved by an orthodox style; continental *puissance* competitions often reach heights of 7 feet with orthodox style—witness also the feats of Captain Piero D'Inzeo at White City in 1957 and 1958—whereas riders adopting the old leave-the-saddle style seldom reach 6 feet. Moreover, this method is usually accompanied in the approach by a good deal of movement, which is not required by the orthodox style described here, which was originated by the Italian Federico Caprilli in about 1904, developed and taught by his pupil, Piero Santini, whose books are still classics on the subject, and taught especially in this country by Colonel Paul Rodzianko and by Captain F. E. Goldman.

Once the rider has achieved his forward position at the take-off, he should follow the movement of the horse over the obstacle with body and hands so as to allow full freedom for the extension of the horse's head and neck. This will vary with the height and spread of the obstacle, and only experience can give the rider the correct 'feels' to enable him to act in harmony with his mount without exaggeration.

When the horse has passed the peak of trajectory of the leap and is about to descend to the landing, he will start to raise his head as a counter-balance to the downward movement. This is where the firm position of the rider in the saddle with calves and knees is essential, so that the hands and body can go back smoothly with the upward movement of the horse's head without losing contact and without getting behind the centre of gravity or falling forward on the horse's neck. The seat should remain out of the saddle, so that the hind feet, legs and quarters have the fullest freedom on landing to propel the horse forward into the normal stride.

If the preliminary stages of training have been carried out correctly and the horse has not been hurried, the pupil horse should pass over these small obstacles without hesitation, with a smooth rounded parabola, without change of speed, head and neck low and extended. If there is a tendency to raise the head and hollow the back, it means that training has been rushed or the rider has been rough with his aids, holding the head too close in and too high. The corrective is plenty of free lane work, and jumping with a rider on his back holding on to a neck-strap only, so as to get him used to the weight of the rider without any accompanying interference.

A tendency to rush at the obstacle can be counteracted in two ways:

(a) Ride the horse normally at the trot towards the fence and turn him away to the right and then left, two strides away from it. Alternate this with riding over the fence.

(b) Place a *cavalletto* in front of the obstacle about three strides from it. If necessary introduce a series of three *cavalletti*.

Refusals at this stage will generally mean that the horse has been over-faced by being brought on too quickly, or has been over-worked at jumping and become fed-up with it. It may also be that the rider's aids at the take-off have not been firm enough.

Firm riding may be the sufficient answer. If not, then stop jumping the horse for about a week and restart at the early stages.

It is very important for both horse and rider that the work up to this stage should be most carefully and patiently carried out, not hurried in any way; it is better to go too slow than too fast. There is one difference here between the human and equine pupils. The rider probably cannot have too much jumping, limited perhaps only by the time of the instructor and the number of trained horses available; though he too must not be taken on too fast. The horse, however, can easily be soured by over-jumping, after which fear is the only instrument available to the trainer instead of co-operation. Thirty to forty-five minutes are ample for a jumping lesson, and three or four days a week should suffice. Regular and prompt reward should accompany all work.

The purpose of these preliminary exercises, which Captain Goldman has called '*passing*' over obstacles rather than '*jumping*' them, is to enable the rider to acquire permanently the '*feels*' of the movement of the horse over an obstacle and to learn to move in harmony with them. The horse learns to approach his jumps quietly and to adjust his strides and balance to the distances and heights. Thus, when they pass on to the advanced stages they will have a firm grounding of elementary education.

Stage 10. Once the instructor is satisfied that work at the trot has stabilized the positions of horse or rider, all the preceding stages should be repeated at the canter.

Stirrup leathers can probably be taken up another one or two holes, so that the rider can take up the correct forward position, which must not be a perched or jockey seat. When at the halt the rider should still be deep in the saddle, but with the knees well forward against the knee rolls of the saddle, leg from knee downwards close to the saddle, knee and toe in a vertical line; heels down without excessive stiffening of the ankles. The rest of the position should be as already described (page 87.)

At the canter, the body should move forward, pivoting on the knees as for a jump, with the seat just off the saddle. Hands should be held low, but not with exaggeration, but on either side of the withers and about level with them. This position gives the necessary freedom to the loins and quarters for the action of the canter and the propulsion for a leap. It also keeps the rider in harmony with the horse and moving with the centre of gravity and not behind it.

As at the trot a steady consistent rhythm should be maintained, keeping up impulsion and increasing it with a squeeze of the legs just before the take-off. With these low obstacles, there should be little change in the canter position during the jump.

As before, the object of all this preliminary work is to perfect the *feels* of movement at the canter and over the obstacles at this new gait, and to unify the movements of horse and rider in one harmonious flow.

The main danger here will be an increased tendency to rush at the fences, which can be prevented to a great extent by the correct transition from trot to canter as has been taught in work on the flat (page 62). Jumping is not an isolated incident in the education of horse and rider but a part of the whole curriculum, and it is important that lessons learned on the flat should not be forgotten when jumping. All turns, circles, halts, etc., should be correctly carried out with the correct aids and bends and flexions.

In stages 8 and 9, if the jumps are movable, their positions should be varied for every lesson. If they are fixed, then it is up to the rider and the instructor to vary the order and direction in which they are taken. Occasionally combine a grid or series of *cavalletti* with the ordinary jumps.

Pupils should not be taken to the next stages until all this work is done smoothly and correctly and the riders' positions are thoroughly stabilized. This is the foundation for the future.

Stage 11. The art of jumping is not learned or taught solely for show jumping in a ring, but so that rider and horse can go freely and safely over any sort of country, primarily in this country when hunting. There is also the sport of cross-country riding (horse trials and combined training to be considered).

A good deal of the work of this stage can be done concurrently with the previous stages. Rides across country should at all times be a feature of training, and horse and rider should be well practised in going over uneven ground and up and down hill before attempting any jumps in the open.

Progress will be conditioned by the land and facilities available, but the more steep slopes and banks that can be provided the better. The rider should be able to walk, trot, and canter over rough ground without losing cadence or impulsion and without being run away with. The horse learns to pick its feet up and be sure-footed over bad surfaces and also to use itself to the full up and down steep declivities. Work over *cavalletti* already described is, of course, an excellent preparation for this.

The rider's position should not alter when going up or down hill, especially the latter, when the tendency is to lean right back. Steep slides and climbs strengthen the horse's leg and back muscles, especially the propelling ones in the quarters. Great care should be taken to avoid hanging on to the horse's mouth in this up-and-down riding, and whether the rider is training or learning, he should have a neck-strap to hang on to if necessary.

The rider's position going down a steep slide has been hotly debated and it is not for me to lay down a hard and fast rule. For short distances the forward position would seem to be better, enabling the rider to free the head and still retain control. On a long and steep decline it may be more effective and more comfortable for the rider to place his centre of gravity directly above that of the horse, which will entail a backward—but not exaggerated—position.

The sequence of riding over obstacles across country should follow the same pattern as that of the previous lessons on the flat: a variety of low jumps taken at the trot and then, when ready, at the canter. The height of the obstacles should not exceed 2 feet 6 inches, spreads not more than 4 feet 6 inches, and all fences should be solid and fixed. It is the greatest mistake to school for cross-country riding over fences that can be knocked down.

The proper execution of this phase is often difficult owing to the lack of facilities. It is easy to describe the ideal requirements here, but few private people or even riding establishments have the space to provide really good cross-country courses. One must make do with whatever means are available, remembering that good cross-country courses are not a substitute for correct basic elementary training.

However, every effort should be made to produce at least one type of obstacle—water. A horse that is used to jumping over or into water is the greatest asset in any sort of competition and in the

91

hunting field. Practise your horse or pony as much as possible over ditches and gaps in the ground of all kinds, with and without water in them, and without guard rails, ground lines or other aids. The little free lane we have spoken about should include an obstacle of this kind.

Stage 12. Cross-country riding is really an endless exercise, which can be carried on concurrently with all future training Although it has been separated here into an isolated stage it should not in fact be treated as such. As well as a means for the rider to apply the riding lessons already learnt, it is a kind of holiday for the horse after the repetitious work in the classroom.

It is now time to repeat the classroom work, however, at greater heights—from 3 feet to 3 feet 6 inches. Once again work progressively at trot and canter. If the preliminary stages have not been hurried, the pupils should be able to take this stage in their stride.

As the jumps are raised—and widened—the greater becomes the necessity for maintaining impulsion without losing the even cadenced flow over a succession of obstacles. The experience and the 'feels' acquired in the previous work should enable the rider to apply the 'squeeze' correctly and at the right instant.

One of the great difficulties in jumping, especially show jumping, is the gauging of the distance in front of the obstacle so as to reach the take-off zone correctly. In the early stages a *cavalletto* five strides before the fence will usually steady the horse and enable him to adjust his stride. Later a mark—a stick, a patch of whitewasn, peg, or some similar indication—will serve as a guide to the rider, so that the necessary 'putting in of short ones' can be done before that point and not just in front of the jump.

This is a counsel of perfection, but worth practising. Show-jumping courses are not straightforward things and of course there are no guide marks on the ground—although the rider can make mental ones when walking the course; you will often find yourself wrong at a jump, in which case the alternatives are to check the horse to make him take a short stride in order to get right again or to leave it to the horse. If he has been trained on the above lines he should more often than not be able to make his own adjustments. Horses have a great capacity for getting themselves and their riders out of trouble! From my own experience and observation and from taking thousands of photographs, I think that the horse has usually made up his mind when he is going to take off before the rider.

It is a good thing at this stage to introduce jumps in combination. As always, start gradually with two low fences placed about five strides apart; gradually reduce the distance to four, three, two and finally one stride. Then vary the heights and nature of the obstacles introducing a spread fence into the combination, as the initial jump and then as the final one.

Stage 13. Transition to this stage will be almost imperceptible. Horse and rider will already have been jumping a variety of obstacles dotted about the training ground. Now these same fences will be placed in a set pattern, to be considered and planned for as a whole.

Start with a simple arrangement, say four or five jumps in an oblong course at equal intervals apart. The rider pupil should walk this course first, pacing out the distances himself, and working out in his mind the spots where he should adjust the approach strides of his horse, if that should be necessary. The fences should be low to begin with—2 feet 6 inches at the most.

Start with a right-handed circuit, and, if the horse completes it smoothly without interruption of cadence at the trot, change the rein and repeat the course the opposite way round. This exercise should be perfected at the trot and then canter before making the course more complicated or raising the height of the fences.

After that progress must depend on the aptness of the pupils and the inventiveness of the instructor. Every course of eight to ten jumps should include at least three spread obstacles of various kinds and, if possible, water. Combinations of two and three fences should, of course, be included, and it is useful sometimes to place a low grid of three, four or five *cavalletti* in the circuit as a steadier for an excitable horse.

The rider should walk the course before jumping it, so that he becomes familiar with distances, the length of his own strides and of his horse and learns to judge them accurately subsequently from the back of the horse.

At this stage the element of time is introduced. The instructor with a stop-watch should time a round several times in order to establish consistency of gait. Then this time can be compared with official speeds, 300 yards a minute and so on, the round to be speeded up or slowed down accordingly.

So far all the jumping has been done at right angles to the obstacle. Now the pupil should practise taking the fences at varying angles and changing direction fairly sharply afterwards. The rider can learn too to circle towards a jump and not away from it, in order to avoid technical refusal faults in show-jumping competitions.

It cannot be stressed too strongly that the rider must not forget his basic equitation and the correct application of the aids between fences and when changing direction. Sudden turns, changes of direction and so on should be produced by the action of the legs and not by pulling about with the reins. Unless the rider's position is orthodox so that his legs are correctly placed to apply the aids, the hands will have to do all the work with resultant bad effect on the horse and the need for drop nose-bands, gags, martingales and all the rest of it. One of the chief faults of the old acrobatic method was that it required a jockey seat, from which the legs were really powerless to help the horse; hence the ugly pulling about of horses' mouths *between* fences in show-jumping arenas.

Stage 14. This is merely a repetition of the work done and a gradual raising of the heights of some of the fences to 4 feet and occasionally to 4 feet 6 inches. The motto here, as always, should be —'No advance without security.' Do not progress unless the previous lesson has been correctly carried out and the way properly prepared for advance.

If show jumping is the ultimate object, occasional greater heights can be jumped, up to 5 feet or so, but never more than once or twice a month. If the horse has been properly and progressively schooled up to normal heights, without ever being over-faced, he will be ready for anything.

Of course things will not always go perfectly. Horses and people are not like that. So much depends on temperament, inherent ability, strength, and conformation. Not every horse or rider is going to reach the final stages of this course; and it is up to the instructor or trainer to discern the limitations at an early stage and set his sights accordingly.

Refusals can be avoided by systematic progress carried out with patience and watchfulness, but they are bound to happen and the trainer must be able to detect whether they spring from wilfulness or from incorrect placing before an obstacle. Some authorities advocate halting the horse and reining him back three or four strides, then driving him forward. Personally, I am in favour of turning him away quietly, with the minimum of rough handling of the mouth, taking a 10-yard circle at his usual pace to bring him straight up to the fence again. He will generally go over.

If the refusal comes towards the end of the lesson, it will probably mean that the horse has had enough of it, and there is no point in having a useless battle. Take him over a low jump and finish for the day. The next day do very little jumping, except over *cavalletti* and low jumps, then start the lessons the day following at the same point as on the day when the trouble occurred.

Horsemastership

The health of the horse plays a greater part in successful training than is often realized. Stable management can make or mar a horse before he ever appears in the manège.

The golden rule is that a horse should have as much exercise as you can give him and as much food as he will eat.

By exercise I mean a period of steady walking and trotting—but mainly walking, carried out every day six days a week. An hour a day, in the morning before school work begins, should be the minimum. An hour's school work after that should be enough for the morning; this work to include at least half an hour of basic training on the flat, with jumping for the last twenty minutes or so.

Then the horse should be watered and fed, and left a long time to digest his meal in peace and quiet. Then there should be grooming and the midday feed. The afternoon pattern of exercise and work should be more or less the same but shorter.

The rules of feeding all lay down little and often, but should be applied with common sense. The facilities available may only permit of three feeds a day—or possibly even two—in which case more time must be given to the horse to digest and absolute quiet during that period. Whatever feeding routine is decided upon must remain consistent and regular.

The only real food for horses is oats; chaff adds the bulk, and bran is a sort of mixing medium with nowadays very little food value. A horse of 16 to 17 h.h. in full work will need between 15 and 16 lb. of oats a day. That is a good figure to start with, to be adjusted according to the individual; the criterion being the health and well-being of the horse and his capacity for work. Add about 3 lb. of bran and 15 lb. of hay. Everything of course must be of the best quality.

This is the behind-the-scenes foundation which can make or mar the work of the best trainer and rider, and it is logically part of the business and art of training a horse to jump—or do anything else for that matter.

6

Practical Applications

Exercise and Bad Habits[1]

'My pony is perfectly quiet at the walk and trot but as soon as I make him canter he begins to buck.' 'My pony won't stand still when mounted.' These and similar problems come up so persistently that one begins to feel that there are an awful lot of bad ponies about! But that, I know, is not the case. There are very few *bad* ponies but far too many badly trained or under-exercised ponies: and under the first heading I include 'badly ridden', which will spoil the best of trained ponies in time.

In dealing with any kind of bad habit the first task is to try and discover its cause. It may take you a long time to do this, but the time spent will not be wasted. Bucking and restlessness may well be due to badly fitting saddlery, for which the remedy is simple. They may be due also to bad treatment at some time or other, which the pony has never forgotten. The cure is to re-establish confidence, which again may be a long business, requiring much patience. Again they may be due to excitement and high spirits, in which case they are only temporary, to be expected and to be got used to.

I am convinced, however, that most of the troubles with ponies are due to under-exercise and over-feeding. I am also convinced that very few people in England nowadays exercise their horses or ponies in such a way as to make them really fit and commensurate with the food they give them to eat. Let us be clear now what we mean by 'exercise'. It is not a day's hunting, or a race, or a game of polo, or a series of show-jumping competitions, any more than playing a Mozart violin concerto at the Festival Hall is doing scales. Exercise is, like musical scales, preparation for these special tasks. It

[1] This section is specially written for children, but the principles are equally applicable to week-end riders of every age.

requires a regular programme, planned according to the particular objective, aimed at whether it be the Derby, Badminton, the Pony Club Championships, a gymkhana, or just the fun of having a quiet, fit horse or pony for all purposes.

The basis of it all is *regular daily work*. To get the best out of your pony you should be able to give it at least one hour's walking and trotting six days a week, quite apart from any schooling. If you are not aiming at any excessive performance in the future, a pony should be able to get fit on this exercise with a normal hay ration, and no oats at all. I am sure that no pony regularly exercised in this way will be an habitual buck jumper or difficult to mount.

It is easy to lay down the correct procedure, but don't tell me how hard it is to apply it—I know! School days make life very difficult for a young pony owner; but school days have to come first —the problem is to adapt the procedure to the circumstances.

For example, if you are not at a boarding school, it may be possible to divide the exercise into morning and evening periods, say 20 minutes or half an hour at a time. If the pony is kept in a big field he will give himself a certain amount of exercise, which you can supplement by a short daily spell; or you can 'let him down' at the beginning of the term—especially if he has had a strenuous time in the holidays—and start getting him fit again after half term. There are various schemes you can adopt, for 'where there is a will there is a way'.

If you are at a boarding school, then it becomes a parental problem. One answer is to allow some child who is not away to exercise it, and this, I think, is a fairly general practice. But you must insist that the basic exercise is regular and according to your plan. There is also no reason why father or mother should not ride the pony, if they can be persuaded to do so; a reasonably sturdy 13 h.h. pony will carry almost any weight at a walk.

Hands and Legs

The aim of all riding is lightness. The very first section of the F.E.I., Rules for Dressage (Chapter 4, Article 3), emphasizes this, speaking of 'the harmony, lightness and ease of the movements', and the 'lightening on the forehand and the engagement of the hindquarters'. Unfortunately so much of the instruction given seems to have the reverse effect. I see more horses and ponies on their forehands, with a strong pull on the reins, in the dressage arena—from Pony Club tests to—yes—Grand Prix, than anywhere else.

A horse or pony can only be *truly* light in hand when he is properly balanced with a rider on his back, who is not hanging on by the reins. Now, with a horse and a grown-up rider who has been properly trained to acquire an independent seat, it is possible to ride lightly with a perfect, gentle, ever-varying contact with the mouth via the reins, without its degenerating into the hard and strong pull which passes so often for 'contact', and leads to so much jargon about 'over the bit', 'under the bit', 'behind the bit', 'in front of the bit', and everywhere you can think of. (What is happening in most cases is that the rider is hanging on by the reins and the horse is trying to escape from this intolerable situation by moving his head about.)

A lot of the trouble with ponies is that instructors try to apply to them and their young riders rules which work all right with horses and adults. But with the former the problem is altogether different. Up to about twelve at all events the young rider has not the strength of leg to hold a pony united and balanced between leg and hand and maintain the ideal slight contact; and the average pony is impervious to such subtleties. The result is bang and pull and very little control.

I suggest that what we should aim at with ponies is getting them to go on a long rein and train them as we would a polo pony. A pony trained like this is never out of control, even though there be no contact with the bit; this is quite different from the pony tucking his head into his chest with the deliberate intention of evading the continuous pull that I have mentioned above. Then he *is* out of control because he has fought you and won. In the former case he has been taught to go that way and understands what it is all about; he is also able to balance himself. This does not contradict anything that has been said about aids, for every pony has to learn them too, and they still have to be applied for certain purposes; the pony that has also learned to go steadily by itself will obey the aids all the more easily and lightly.

The way to teach the pony to go on a long rein is to ride him in the school on a fairly big circle, say 20 yards diameter. Walk him round and gradually reduce the contact, which with most ponies is pretty heavy, but do not relax the pressure of your legs in an invitation to go slower. You want him to walk round at the same pace, neither more nor less. He will try and go faster and instead of doing what you usually do—pull harder—relax the rein still more (you do this by moving your hands forward, *not* letting the reins slide through your fingers) and keep up the leg action. Don't hold him in, but keep him on the circle by a gentle indication with the inside rein. Once he finds there is nothing to pull against he will begin to slow down; now things are beginning to happen! Take the opportunity of adjusting your position which has probably become unbalanced with the effort of pushing him on. The next thing to do is to keep him going on at the same pace until *you* want to slow down. Then, instead of yielding with your hands as you have been doing, hold them steady so that the pony comes up against the bit, which he will take as the signal to slow down. Once you have achieved this you will have gone a long way towards the mastery of your pony and greater comfort in riding for both of you.

It will not happen all at once. The pony is probably so used to pulling on the bit that at first when he comes up against the fixed hand he will start to pull and go fast. Your reaction is once more to yield the hand so that he has nothing to pull against and to make him keep up his speed. Continual repetition will do the trick.

For Gymkhana and Polo Ponies

More rosettes are won outside the show ring than in it is an old and well-proved saying. Whether you are going in for jumping, show classes, best-rider classes, or gymkhana events, it is always the efficiency and care of the preparation—that is to say preliminary training—that counts. You cannot wait to begin training your pony until you get into the show ring.

If all the foundation work that has been described in these pages has been done carefully and patiently, you should be in a position to apply it for really practical purposes—for gymkhanas, show jumping, riding tests, polo or what you will. As has been emphasized already, the essence of successful and comfortable riding is lightness, handiness and obedience. The emphasis on contact has generally resulted in a loss of lightness, which is deplorable.

The exercises that I am going to describe are simply a rearrangement and re-application of all the work that has been done in a more advanced and specialized manner.

You can work in a manège or any quiet field, provided you mark out an area approximately 20 yards by 40 yards and keep within it. The work can be done by yourself or in company with two or three other riders, in which case all must conform to the commands of the leader.

For the first two or three lessons just do quiet ordinary riding-school work. At the walk and trot do simple turns on the move across the school, then circles on either rein, changes of rein, and finally large figures of eight (at a walk and trot only.) Mix this up with halting while on the move, and turns on the haunches at the halt.

All this time ride him at attention but without excessive use of the legs—just moderate pressure, and with as light hands on the reins as possible. More often than not the task will be to raise the pony's head and lighten the forehand rather than the reverse; so it is quite all right to keep your hands higher than usual, and generally play with the pony's mouth. Never let him get his head down and weigh down his forehand in this period. The purpose is to exercise his muscles and supple him up and get him used to the aids quietly and correctly applied.

I should not let these lessons last longer than half an hour; then you can go for a quiet hack, during which you might have a bit of a canter, but if you can restrain your ardour so much the better. There will be plenty of time for cantering and galloping later on, but now the quieter you keep your pony the better, so that he and you can concentrate on obedience to the aids and lightness of mouth and forehand. One thing you must remember all the time is to do everything *equally* to left or right; don't favour one side only because it happens to be easier.

After seven to ten lessons of this kind—you must judge for yourself so far as you can when the pony is performing all the movements correctly (or as correctly as possible) and promptly (that is the important thing)—you can start the next stage. For this you want to use the end of the school only, making a circle of about 6 yards radius.

Start at a slow, well collected trot. Trot round once or twice quietly, then cross over and change the rein and again trot round once or twice. Change the rein again and halt. Rein back three paces, then forward again into a collected trot. Now you must start using your legs strongly but still quietly. If you have a pony which won't do this without continual banging with the legs, you must get somebody stronger to ride him for a bit.

Now you are back, say on the right rein, trot round, bumping in the saddle, again three or four times and do a series of half-halts. A half-halt is really a very quick halt—stop and on again before the pony has time to relax and his hocks are still well under him. The aids for the halt are applied with greater firmness and suddenness. Very strong leg action is required, and a quick action on the mouth, immediately to be relaxed as the pony obeys. With a horse that habitually keeps its head down, the rein action can be upwards as well; one of the results of these exercises is to get ponies and horses off their forehand.

The moment the pony has come to a halt and the reins are relaxed the legs must drive him forward again into the same collected trot. Repeat the same lesson on the left rein; and make sure that you do the same number of half-halts on that rein as you did on the right.

Then halt, drop your reins and sit at ease, and pat your pony and generally make much of him.

Don't relax too long, but get cracking again and repeat the same lesson; then again you can give him a rest and a pat, and, if you like, a titbit—*provided* he has done the work correctly. You want great patience here, because you should not go on until the pony is completely obedient to hands and legs in this exercise.

If all has gone well, you can mix the half-halts with full-halts, rein-back, and turns on the haunches (the last to be done when you want to change the rein instead of crossing over diagonally). At first these turns can be done slowly, but the aim is to quicken them up so that the pony learns to turn directly the aid is applied after the halt, and finally when a neck-rein aid only is given.

Don't carry these lessons on for more than half an hour; give less time at first if the pony responds. It is hard work for both of you, and if you have done it properly you will be quite tired at the end; but, apart from training the pony, it is first-rate work for you, exercising all your riding muscles, and strengthening your grip. At the end of each lesson give the pony a bending lesson for a few minutes; shoulder in and shoulder out one day; half-pass the next. But the important thing is suppling and lightening work on the circle.

After about a week, again, if all is well, you can spend half the time doing the same work at the slow, collected canter. It is very important that all this work is done collectedly. Take the greatest care to see that the pony always canters true and don't attempt any other work until that matter is settled. Remember always that you do not take a step forward until the last step has been taken correctly.

Towards the end of the second week you should be able to quicken the halts and turns, remembering always that you must move forward again into the same pace as when you stopped: if you halt at the canter, then the pony must spring forward again into the canter. He will be awfully inclined at first to trot a bit; this is where your legs come in, insisting on obedience. Incidentally, when you are doing your turns, don't always turn inwards towards the centre of the circle but outwards towards the circumference. Most ponies will object to doing this, and again this is where you impose discipline and obedience. The great thing is to have variety: first a half-halt, then a hlt and turn to the right, then a half-halt, then a halt and rein back, then a halt and turn outwards—just when master pony, the imp, is thinking you are going to do another half-halt. Ponies will slide into a routine very quickly if you let them.

For the fourth week—and the fifth if you have time for that—

you can spend all the time at the canter after a preliminary minute or two at the collected trot, just for running in as it were. Now you can quicken the pace and use the whole school. But never let the pony get extended and out of hand; always keep him collected. In these last periods, also, do a lot of the work with the reins in one hand so that the pony learns to respond to neck-reining, and yet is under control by the legs. This will stand you in good stead in many a gymkhana.

At the end of this time your pony should be light on the bit and obedient to the aids. Do not expect too much, however, at first; ponies' mouths are often very hard and need a lot of reconditioning. But this is the way to do it, as I have proved on many a polo pony with a ruined mouth. The whole programme is progressive, and of course the length of it must vary with almost every pony. So do not be disappointed if the progress is slow and the pony is not perfect by the first show of the year. So long as some progress has been made all is well, and the lessons can go on all through the year; indeed they should go on a couple of lessons a week at least, all through the season.

Polo Practice

Polo is a bat-and-ball game, with the added complication of having to hit the ball with a mallet at the end of a whippy cane about six feet away from the eye, while you, the mount and the ball are travelling at about thirty miles an hour over a bumpy surface with somebody trying hard to prevent you.

After horsemanship, teamwork, and pony power have been taken into consideration, the fact remains that the essence of polo is stick-work. No amount of intelligent placing of players is any good if the ball cannot be hit towards the required position. The fastest pony in the world is useless if you cannot hit the ball when it gets you to it ahead of your opponent.

The foundations of polo horsemanship are the same as for any other equestrian activity. The more independent the seat the better, given a good eye and a supple wrist, will be the stick work. The aim of polo pony training is to make it light in hand, have it well on its hocks and yet full of forward impetus. The position of the rider should be well forward, with shortish stirrup leathers; this enables the body, the knee the pivot as in jumping, to bend well down to hit the ball; it also keeps the weight off the loins, expecially when the pony is using its hocks for stopping, turning and springing off again, or when it is being swung round on a very small circle.

To return to stick work. The first thing, naturally, is to have a stick, or mallet, which suits you. A good deal of this is personal preference. I used to prefer a cylindrical head to a cigar—or square-shaped-one, because I thought it had more hitting surface and driving power, but I have come to the conclusion there was nothing in it. Some people like split-cane handles, others single cane, some very whippy, some very stiff. The best is what suits the individual best, and you can only find out by trial and error.

The length of the shaft requires more thought. I am definitely of the opinion that the shorter a stick a player can use the better he will be. To begin with, you are nearer the ball and so have a better chance of keeping your eye on it. Next, the stick is lighter and more manageable in a mêlée or for a quick push in front of goal. The short stick makes you bend down and really look at the ball. This again makes you adopt a more forward position than you would with a longer stick, which may well give you that vital advantage at the start of a gallop or at a turn.

The combination of forward position and short stick makes it much easier to hit the ball at the best moment when it is level with the pony's forefoot as it reaches the ground. The tendency of most beginners—and others too, who ride long—is to hit the ball too far back and so dig at it, losing all the value of swing and timing

Too short a shaft, however, makes a backhand stroke more difficult; or it requires more suppleness of body to reach down for it. In this case the best moment for striking the ball is when it is level with the hindfoot of the pony touching the ground. It is up to the individual player to find his own optimum length.

There are various ways of holding the stick, and I have seen the best players use all kinds of grips; it must be a firm one, round the top of the handle, the thumb pressed straight along the side giving direction. Generally speaking, hold the polo stick as you would a racquet.

Accuracy comes from concentration and closeness to the ball. Length comes from swing and timing and the snap given at the moment of impact by a strong, supple wrist. Some people can use their forearms and clout the ball as if they had a hammer in their hands, but swing and wrists come easier for most.

Accuracy and length are the two things to aim at; and the first essential is accuracy. Length is easy if you have a reasonably supple wrist and a good eye.

A polo pit and wooden horse are essential for the first polo lessons, as well as for practice at all times; but they need to be used with circumspection. Hours of wild hitting at the ball from all angles do little good.

Do not have a ball at all to begin with. Just sit, get accustomed to the feel of the mallet in your hands and to its weight and distance from the ground. Swing it freely but quietly round and round so that it just touches the ground in passing. Have a mark on the ground with what would be the point of contact of the pony's off-fore with the ground, and keep your eye on that mark all the time you are swinging.

The base from which you swing—and eventually hit—is the triangle made by the knees, heels and stirrups, which takes all your weight when the stroke is made; you lean forward and down as much as is necessary to reach the ball. The left hand should be forward on the pony's neck; it is a good thing always, whether playing or practising, to use a neck-strap to hang on to when reaching for a distant ball, which is preferable to using the pony's mouth as a hook. Leathers should not be as short as they would be for jumping, but short enough to enable you to keep your heels down and the lower part of your leg just behind the perpendicular. In the swing, the shaft and the head will always just follow the hand and the arm, not go as a continuation of them.

In the polo pit for the first time, swing half a dozen times on the offside—for the normal forehand shot—then switch over to the nearside and swing again six times for the nearside forward shot, which is the equivalent of a backhander in tennis or racquets; hold the stick in the same way, back of the hand to the front. You will find that you have to bend appreciably more to reach the ground on that side; make sure that you do get low enough. It is worth while practising more on this side than on the offside, so take another six swings, before coming back to the offside for the normal backhand stroke, again holding the mallet as for a tennis backhand. Take six swings, then over to the nearside for the back stroke, which is really a forehand stroke, the mallet held in the same way as for the offside forward shot; six swings again. Repeat this sequence, with occasional rests, for about half an hour. The object is to produce suppleness of waist and hips and shoulders and a free straight swing on both sides of the horse.

Make sure that the head of the stick is facing to the front at right angles to the line of the ball (you hit the ball with the flat long side on the mallet, not the end as in croquet); the first job is to learn to hit the ball straight. Stop your swing at its lowest point every now and then to check its position. About a week of this and you will be able to take a ball.

The proper polo pit is so made that after being hit the ball eventually runs back down the slope to the lowest point where the horse is, thus enabling you to practise hitting a moving ball coming at all angles. But the time for that is not yet.

Concentrate on the swing and the straightness of the mallet; do not attempt to hit the ball hard. If you find yourself slicing, you are (*a*) taking your eye off the ball; (*b*) dropping your shoulder; (*c*) holding the stick crooked; (*d*) pressing. You will know when the timing is right, for the ball will shoot off the head of the stick with a clean crisp click and a drive that is unmistakable.

For the first few lessons concentrate on hitting a stationary ball *straight* ahead of you. Put a mark on the wall of the pit in front of you, and another behind, and aim at that every time you hit the ball. After hitting, let the ball come back and place it correctly with your mallet for the next shot. When you can hit that mark or get very near it five times out of six from all four directions, then you can tackle more difficult shots.

These are the cut and the pull. To cut you simply turn the head of your stick as you bring it down so that it hits the ball facing the way you want it to go. Start with a narrow cut, say 30 degrees, and as before have a mark to aim at. Go through the same sequence as before, off and near side, until you have become reasonably accurate at all angles. The wider the cut the further must the ball be from the side of the pony.

Repeat the process for the pull shot; remember that the sharper the pull, the lower must you bend the body, and the ball should be taken further in front of the pony than for an ordinary forward or cut shot. For the backward shots ,the ball, of course, must be taken clear of the pony's hind legs.

When you have got reasonable control of these basic strokes, it is time to work from the back of a real horse. The ideal practice is at full speed, but few people have the ponies to spare for this. The following practice has been found useful both for the beginner and the experienced player, and can be carried out in a small area without excessive wear and tear on the horse.

Any field of moderately flat surface will do, about the size of a football ground, or less if need be. Collect as many old polo balls as you can up to twenty and set them out in a row about 5 feet apart. Get two poles and set them up 60 yards from the row of balls, or as far as space will allow. The regulation goal width is 24 feet, but set these 10 or 12 feet apart; when eventually you face a real goal the opening will seem enormous!

Canter round smoothly on a nice big circle so that you approach the row of balls on a straight line to the goal mouth. Do a few preliminary circles to get used to the rhythm of the movement and get the timing of your swing. Then, starting with the offside forward shot, quietly hit all the balls one after the other at and if possible through the goal posts. Concentrate on a nice, smooth swing and on the timing of the stroke. This is also a good training exercise for a future polo pony, giving him the best kind of stick-and-ball practice. Don't worry about distance, the great thing is direction. Far more heinous faults are to top the ball or get underneath it.

The only arduous part of this lesson is the collection of the balls and re-laying them for the next stroke—nearside forward shot. So you proceed through the range of the strokes.

You can vary your angles and distance and perfect your timing and aim, working for an hour or more without unduly tiring the pony or knocking it about.

Once this foundation is securely laid, you can go into fast work and polo games with considerable confidence. The accuracy you have gained will never desert you.

Hard Cases

In the preceding pages it has generally only been possible to lay down general principles, although illustrated in the main by actual cases. The application of these principles is not simple, because every actual experience is always just a little different, making it not easy to recognize the principle involved. So I have taken a number of genuine and most frequent enquiries on different equestrian subjects, which I have received and answered in the magazine *Pony*, referring back where necessary to the relevant pages of this book.

Low head carriage

Q. My pony carries his head very low when out hacking. I wonder if you could advise me how to bring it into the correct position?
—J. W.

A. Low head carriage generally means that the pony is on its forehand and not properly balanced. It may also come from weakness in the muscles of the neck, through unfitness and lack of proper training. The basic cause of the trouble is weak leg action and hanging on with the reins. If the pony is young, I would suggest retraining from the start with regular work on the lunge as the foundation. Riding exercise should be carried out with a strong rider using his legs strongly and holding his hands higher than normal, so as to gradually raise the pony's head when the legs drive him forward. Hands must never be allowed to pull backwards, but to keep upwards and remain steady while the leg action gets the pony's hindquarters active and more under the body, which will eventually lighten the forehand and bring the centre of gravity back a little. A lot of work should be done in the school on a large circle at walk and trot, and later at the canter with a half-halt and halt and turn, working on each rein with a strong leg action as possible and a light hand; gradually the horse will come up and his mouth may become softer. (Page 99.)

Reining back

Q. My bay mare—12.3 h.h.—is very good except for reining back, when she throws her head around and runs back zig-zagging. She does this even if I give her the lightest of aids. How can I prevent her from doing this?—B. T.

A. It may well be that her teeth are hurting her or her gums are sore. Have the mouth examined by a vet. As she appears to have no actual objection to going back, try making her go back from the ground. Invite her to go back one step only, then stop her and reward her and gradually get her used to going back one step at a time. When mounted, try a rubber or vulcanite half-moon snaffle, and apply aids as follows: From the halt, press with your legs quietly but firmly, as if giving the aid for the walk, but do not give with your hands; instead, hold them still so that the pony wants to move forward but is stopped by the bit, so there is nothing for her to do but go back. The pressure of your legs will keep her up to the bit and straight. Don't pull backwards with your hands at all at first, though a gentle vibration of the fingers may be necessary. Once the pony has gone back one step, relax and make much of her. Repeat this at intervals during a ride, and gradually ask her to take two or more steps, but not until she takes the first step properly and quietly. (Page 72.)

Sluggish pony

Q. My pony is a very slow starter. I kick so as to make him leap into action, but all he does is amble along at a slow walk. I find this very uncomfortable when he is heading for a jump, because he does not jump it properly. This fault is not through being over or under fed, nor tiredness. My pony is three years old.—C. B.

A. The pony is still very young and it looks as if training has been rushed and he has been ridden too soon. He is probably not

107

muscled up or properly fit. I suggest you start re-training with work on the lunge (page 26), and try adding a handful of oats to his daily feed, or horse nuts or cubes. (Page 119.)

Up to the bit

Q. Could you please tell me how to make a horse come on to his bit?
M. O.

A. Use your legs with a steady pressure and keep your hands still.

Head shaking

Q. I have bought a 13-h.h. six-year-old pony who has not been ridden for a long time. I have started schooling her for jumping over poles but she still persists in shaking her head vigorously when I begin to do anything, e.g. trot, canter, etc. What shall I do?

A. A possible cause for the head shaking, if you are satisfied that the bridle, etc. fit properly, may be bad teeth or soreness in the mouth, so you should have her mouth examined by a vet. If this is all right, try her in a half-moon rubber or vulcanite snaffle and a drop nose-band—but get someone to show you the correct fitting. (*See* page 50.) When riding her, you must use your legs strongly to drive her forward up to the bit, and you must keep up the leg pressure to prevent her getting her head free from the restraint of the bit, which is when she can resist you by head shaking.

Over-jumping

Q. How can I cure a pony from taking a huge leap over quite a small jump? And what would the cause be?—Y. J.

A. It is difficult to tell what the cause of your pony jumping high is, knowing nothing about her previous history. Very possibly she has had a fall at a jump in the past and is taking no risks. The best thing to do is to train her, first of all unmounted and then mounted, over a grid, that is, a series of small jumps placed quite close together (*cavalletti*). They should not be more than 8–10 inches high. To begin with they should be placed about 3 feet apart and you should try and walk her over them. Then extend them to about 4 feet apart and trot her over them. She should begin to improve if you persevere in this way. The distances given are only approximate, and depend on the size of the pony. A little trial and error will give you the right intervals for your pony. Do all your jumping practice at the trot. (Ch.V)

Bridling

Q. My pony often refuses to be bridled. He throws his head up, bares his teeth, and backs away. Could you please advise me what to do?—G. S.

A. First of all have his mouth and teeth inspected. He may have a bad tooth or sore gums, which make the bit painful to him. If this is all right, he has probably been roughly bridled while being trained and has never forgotten it. Or he may be just naughty, having discovered that he can stop you bridling him. In either case, you will have to avoid any roughness or attempt to force him, or bumping the bit against his front teeth. Practise bridling him when you are not actually going for a ride. First of all, take the chill off the bit in warm water. Then rub it over with sugar, while the bit is slightly damp. Let the pony get the taste of that and he will probably lower his head to investigate and get some more. While he is doing this, put the reins over his head and slip your fingers into his mouth at the corners of the lips, between the bars, which will make him open it, when you should be able to get the bit in all right. Be very quiet and patient and you should break down his resistance.

Mounting trouble

Q. Please can you give me some advice on teaching my pony to stand while being mounted?—A. J.

A. You need a helper to hold the pony while you mount and when you have mounted and the pony has stood still, then the assistant should immediately reward her with some titbit that she likes. If she will not stand still at first and struggles against the assistant walk her round two or three times and then start again. You must just persevere until you can mount without her pulling against the assistant so that she learns to understand that standing still brings reward. If you can arrange it, try using a mounting block. (Page 39.)

109

Tongue out

Q. How can you stop a pony sticking his tongue out? And why does he do it? He is ridden in a drop nose-band.—H. C.

A. The first thing to do is to inspect his mouth very carefully. The bars on that side may be sore and he is putting out his tongue as a protection. He may be a bit one-sided and you should concentrate for a while on doing a lot of work to the opposite side—circles, bending, and so forth, and also using the opposite diagonal when trotting. All these little things affect the horse and this may be his reaction to it. I should also try using a rubber or vulcanite bit with a half-moon mouthpiece.

Canter

Q. How can I teach my six-year-old mare to lead with her off fore at the canter? She very much favours the near fore.—H. O.

A. Try the following exercise: Ride a sitting trot on a circle to the right—20 yards diameter—and gradually make the circle smaller and smaller. When you have been round about three times, reducing the diameter to 10–12 yards—keep hold of *both reins* firmly and go on reducing the circle; as you do this give the aids for the canter. After a few steps, stop, and repeat the exercise two or three times. Do this every day for at least seven days, and you should get her going right.

Ticklish

Q. My pony kicks and refuses to have her mane and tail plaited or pulled. What can I do, as they are badly in need of doing?—S. J.

A. Get somebody to hold up one forefoot while the job is being done. Start on the mane first; begin by using the brush only, then try plaiting; but do not attempt pulling at first. Reward her at once. It is more than likely that the hairs of the mane and tail have been roughly pulled, several at a time, so get her used to brushing and plaiting first.

Bitting problem

Q. My pony is five years old, 14 h.h. He is half Arab and half Welsh. I ride him in a pelham with a vulcanite mouthpiece. When out riding he keeps fidgeting with his bit, putting his tongue over it, then under it, and so on. He seems to be uncomfortable, and I would be very pleased and relieved if you could tell me what the matter is and what I can do about it.—R. H.

A. Have you inspected your pony's mouth very carefully for any possible sore place on the bars or gums? If not, get a vet to inspect the mouth and the teeth, because, if there is anything wrong there, that may be the cause of your trouble. If all is well there, try a snaffle bit with a thick rubber or vulcanite mouth-piece (half-moon not jointed), and tie a leather bootlace, crossed in his mouth, between the rings of the bit and the nose-band; that will keep his tongue in place.

7

Horsemastership

The Fit Horse and the Sick Horse

The whole object of horsemastership is to keep your horse fit and well. So let us have a look at a healthy horse.

When the Horse is Well

The healthy horse or pony stands squarely and firmly on all four feet, occasionally resting one hind foot on the toe. *If it rests a fore foot something is wrong*. The head is alert, eyes wide open, and ears pricking backwards and forwards. The coat is sleek and shiny and the skin loose and supple. The colour of the lining of the eyes and nostrils is a healthy salmon pink. The pulse is about forty, breathing fifteen to the minute, and normal temperature 100–101·5 degrees. The bowels are moved frequently—average eight times in twenty-four hours; droppings should be of good consistency, golden yellow to dark green 'when much green food is being taken), not slimy and should break as they reach the ground. Urine is thick in appearance, light yellow in colour, and is passed several times a day, about a quart at a time. Don't mistake the grunting and straddling position assumed on those occasions for pain.

Signs of Ill Health

Droppings may be hard and constipated or loose and watery. The coat is dull and staring. The lining of the eyes and nostrils may be a bad colour—very pale, or dark red, or yellowish and spotted. The animal may be listless, obviously off colour, and off his feed. He may be resting a fore leg, due to pain somewhere in the leg or foot, which will cause lameness. These signs may be present singly or in combination; they may be only temporary, but they are danger signals which need immediate attention.

112

When In Doubt Consult a Vet

Simple First Aid Notes

Test the breathing—from the movement of the nostrils or the rise and fall of the flanks. (Practise this when the horse is healthy so that any deviation from normal is quickly recognized.) Feel the pulse under the lower jaw. Take the temperature. Shake the thermometer well, grease the mercury end, and insert it into the anus gently; keep it in two or three minutes, then take the reading and write it down, noting date and time. Then shake down the mercury again, wash the thermometer carefully and put away. If the horse is pointing his foot make tests for lameness (*see below*).

Equine indisposition normally comes under four main headings: Fever, indigestion, lameness and wounds.

Fever. Usually a symptom of something else, though it occasionally appears temporarily on its own. General symptoms: temperature well over 101·5 degrees; breathing and pulse above normal; constipation; urine highly coloured and scanty; staring coat and shivering.

Immediate action: Keep warm with plenty of rugs and bandages; take off all work; reduce diet and restrict to mashes and boiled foods; give a purgative, and plenty of water, and have green food available for him to eat if he wants it. *If the horse is not better in twenty-four hours call in the vet.*

Indigestion. The cause of colic (stomach-ache) is mostly wrong diet and bad stable management. It may also be the result of crib-biting or wind-sucking.

General symptoms: Horse is ill-at-ease and keeps looking round at his flanks; tendency to lie down and roll; hindlegs stamp and kick at the belly to try and get rid of the pain. Patches of sweat may appear with fast pulse and breathing. Temperature remains normal. Colic appears usually in two forms; spasmodic and windy. In the former the pain is violent but intermittent; in the latter pain is continuous but not violent, accompanied by distension of the stomach; the horse appears sleepy, wants to lie down but is afraid to do so, is restless and fidgety. Acute constipation is present in both varieties.

Immediate action: Keep the horse quiet and warm. If he is very restless, walk him about and prevent him lying down, which may cause rupture in the bowel. Some people say this is not necessary, but it is as well to be on the safe side. Relieve pain with a prepared colic drink; administer copious enemas every half-hour to remove constipation. If no relief in a couple of hours call the vet. In an emergency give brandy, rum or whisky—half a tumbler, but colic drinks should always be kept available ready made up.

Lameness. Main causes: sprains and strains of muscles and ligaments, inflamation of bones (splints), wounds, faulty shoeing. Most common seats of lameness are the feet and the legs below the knees; lameness at the shoulder or hip is comparatively rare.

General symptoms: pointing the fore foot while at rest (of course, not applicable to the hind feet); favouring the lame foot while on the move; heat and swelling and the presence of pain if the part is touched or moved.

Immediate action is to locate the seat of lameness, by trial and error. Take off work and reduce food. The general treatment for sprains is the application of pressure bandages and massage (nowadays radio-therapy is applied in some big stables but is still too expensive for general use).

Sudden lameness while riding may be caused by a stone stuck in the frog, the removal of which ends the lameness. Other causes of lameness in the feet are pricks, while shoeing or by something picked up on the move, pressure on the sole causing bruising or corns, neglect to keep clean (causing thrush), underwork and overfeeding (causing laminitis), diseases of the navicular and sesamoid bones. In every case have shoes removed and send for the vet.

Wounds. May be clean-cut, lacerated, bruised, or punctured. The most frequent and most troublesome are bruised wounds—e.g. broken knees, over-reaches, treads, saddle and girth galls.

Immediate action: Wash and keep clean. Wash out open wounds with cold running water to get rid of all dust and mud. Once the wound is clean, dry all the surrounding part thoroughly, apply some antiseptic-sulphanilamide, Dettol, or iodine, and cover with a loosely fixed piece of lint, tied above the wound so that it hangs down over it, to keep flies and dirt away. If there is much bleeding it will be either venous—a steady flow, which is stopped eventually by direct pressure; or arterial—in copious spurts with fountain force, in which case a tourniquet is applied between the heart and the wound to close the artery and stop the flow. In the case of a bad wound, a cut artery, or a wound near a joint, send for the vet.

Flies. All flies and gnats worry ponies, but two of the most troublesome are the warble and the bot fly.

The *warble fly* lays her eggs on the coat, often on the back where the saddle goes. The eggs hatch out and the maggots burrow under the skin. The first sign of trouble is a lump, which eventually breaks as the warble comes through.

Treatment is either to foment the lump at its first appearance, or to leave it until the hole is made, then squeeze the warble out and apply some iodine.

The *bot fly* lays her eggs in the long hairs inside the knee and forearm of the horse or pony. Eventually the pony licks them off, swallows them, and the grubs hatch out in the stomach, where they stay for the winter. Unless in great numbers they are not particularly harmful, and it takes very drastic drugs to get rid of them.

Prevention is the answer here. First of all regular supervision. As soon as the yellow specks, which are the eggs, are noticed on the pony's legs, scrape them off the legs with an old, blunt safety razor.

A type of gnat lays its eggs inside the pony's ears, which become raw and painful. The first sign is the pony shaking its head a lot and objecting to being bridled. Always inspect the ears when this occurs.

Treatment is to smear with vaseline two or three times a week.

All ponies suffer from red worms and a heavy worm burden can cause severe debility and even death. For this reason ponies should be given a worm dose at least twice a year, but under veterinary supervision.

The Medicine Cupboard

Don't make a chemist's shop of it! Keep the contents down to a necessary minimum of basic equipment and immediate remedies.

Equipment: Spare rug; thermometer; antiseptic lint, 1 roll; cotton wool, 1 roll; tow; surgical bandages (3-inch), several rolls; crêpe bandages (3-inch), 2 rolls; oiled silk; scissors; forceps; kidney-shaped basin, and several other enamel basins of various sizes; drenching bottle (use a plastic squash bottle); enema syringe; dropper; dusters; towels; sponges; rubber gloves.

Medicines. Linseed oil (medicinal); turpentine (medicinal); vaseline; boracic powder; sulphanilamide powder; disinfectant and anti-septics; gall cure; iodine; permanganate of potash; lead lotion; carbolic soap; antiphlogistine; colic drench, ready mixed; zinc ointment; cold and cough electuary; Stockholm tar; embrocation. Things like worm powders can always be bought as required. Go over the medicine cupboard periodically to check what is there.

Giving a horse a ball. An assistant holds the horse's head on the offside. Standing on the nearside, take hold of the tongue gently with the left hand, turning it upwards so that it makes the mouth open; with the right hand push the ball as far as possible over the root of the tongue down the throat. It can be seen going down the gullet if swallowed; if not, give a drink of water or some green grass.

Drenching. A drench is a liquid physic ball given to relieve colic. An assistant holds the horse's head well up; then stands on a firmly based stool or box and pours down from the drenching-bottle in a slow trickle, with frequent pauses for swallowing.

Electuary. This is a cough mixture mixed with honey. It is administered by rubbing the mixture on the tongue from a wooden spoon or flat narrow piece of wood. A wooden spoon with the sides cut off is the most effective instrument.

Constipation is caused by too much dry food, too little exercise, or too little water. Epsom salts and bran mashes are the immediate remedy.

Diarrhoea is brought on by too much work, too much soft green food and by the horse being cold. Rest him, keep him warm, feed dry bran.

Send for the vet at once if your horse has colic, fever, swelling on the withers or poll, a bad wound near a joint, any discharge from nostrils, eyes or mouth, or if he is very lame.

Enema. Should be given cold and copiously. Don't forget to grease the nozzle first.

Prevention is better than cure
The best preventatives of illness are proper, regular feeding with food of the best quality, and sufficient regular exercise.

Do not water or work directly after feeding, or colic will result.

Do not underwork and overfeed your horse.

Do not fail to keep the feet and clefts of the frogs clean and dry.

Do not keep your horse in an overheated, stuffy stable; or in a draughty one.

Do not keep your horse standing about after he has got very hot.

Do not ride him to the point of exhaustion.

Feeding

Fitness depends largely on correct feeding and correct feeding depends on common sense and daily supervision. The phrase 'the eye of the master makes the horse fat' means that the eye should see at once if the horse is losing condition—or conversely getting too fat—and arrange the diet accordingly. (It also used to mean seeing that the grooms did not pinch the corn!)

The staple foods of the horse are grass, hay (either long or as chaff or chopped hay), oats, bran (as a makeweight and mixing medium for the other things). The horse will eat all sorts of other things—barley, maize, brewer's grains, and so on, but they can only be regarded as substitutes if the staple items are not available.

Basic principles

1. Keep water available at all times.
2. Feed in small quantities and often.
3. Do not work immediately after a full feed.

Ponies

Native pony breeds all over the world thrive very well on grass and hay. Only in exceptional circumstances when they are asked to do long and heavy work should they be given corn. Ponies ridden only by children only get above themselves and develop unpleasant tricks if given oats.

For a pony that lives out the grazing will be the foundation, supplemented as necessary by hay and bran and roots. A stable-kept pony will need more of the latter. Possibly before hunting or a strenuous gymkhana a feed of oats may be given. The amount of hay will vary from ten to twelve pounds daily, according to the size and condition of the pony. Generally give as much hay as he will eat, but watch the grazing, for too much good green grass will make the pony over-fat and may affect his wind. Some of the hay can be fed as chaff mixed with bran and roots—apples, carrots, turnips, mangolds, and so on, giving variety to the diet according to season. The ration should be bran up to two pounds and roots up to four pounds. Cut all roots longways. If oats are given the amount should average three or four pounds, and not exceed five or six pounds.

Pony nuts are an even more convenient way of feeding and can be substituted for oats or roots. Three to four pounds is a sufficient quantity for a pony that is not in hard and regular work.

Horses

Oats are the best food for horses in hard work. The amount given depends on each individual horse, its size, work, and temperament. The following quantities are average and can be taken as a rough guide, and they are for horses in full hard work:

Height	Oats	Bran	Hay	
Up to 15 h.h.	10–12 lb.	2 lb.	10–12 lb.	(Chaff 5 lb.)
15–16 h.h.	12–15 lb.	2–3 lb.	12 lb.	(Chaff 5 lb.)
16–17 h.h.	15–16 lb.	3 lb.	15 lb.	(Chaff 8 lb.)

117

Racehorses in full training are given as much oats as they can eat
—about 22 lb. But the maximum for other horses is about 18 lb.

Feeding Routine

The total ration should be divided between three to four meals. If
the former, then each feed will be larger and longer time must be
allowed for digestion—a minimum of one hour. The times of feeding
depend on circumstances and work to be done, but on a normal
four-meal basis they may be: Morning, 9 a.m.; midday, 12 noon to
1 p.m.; afternoon, 5 p.m.; evening as late as possible. On a hunting
day the morning meal would be later and the midday feed on
return. Always give fresh long hay before morning exercise, and in
the afternoon between feeds.

If the horse does not finish a feed it usually means he is having
too much at a time. Cut down the individual feed but add an extra
meal to the day so that the total remains the same. If you have to
increase the horse's total feed, do not increase the individual meals
but add an extra meal on.

Always see that the stable is absolutely quiet after each feed so
that digestion can take place in peace and efficiently.

Preparation of Meals

All corn given must be perfectly clean and free from dust, grit, and
other foreign bodies; sieve it if possible. Good quality oats should
have short and plump grains with a healthy sunburnt colour, hard
and dry and odourless. Meals should be prepared on a table on
a movable piece of American cloth or paper, so that all split grains
can be preserved and not allowed to go to the floor to attract rats.
Wash your hands before mixing. Measure out the oats into a deep
bowl, add a couple of good handfuls of chaff and mix well. Then
add the same amount of bran and again mix thoroughly, sprinkling
with water so that the mixture is just slightly damp. If roots are
given at the same time, slice longways and add to the mixture.

Mashes and Gruels

Bran mash is a mild laxative given every week in practically every
stable before a no-work day. Pour boiling water on to about 3 lb. of
bran and mix well, with some Epsom salts added, until it is a light
paste. Cover the bucket and leave for about 15 minutes until cool
enough to eat. Serve last thing at night and prepare just before you
serve it—not hours before.

Linseed mash is good for fattening a horse in bad condition.

Boil 1-1½ lb. linseed slowly for about three hours, until the grains are soft. There should be enough water over to soak up about 1 lb. bran. Add this bran paste to the linseed when it is cooked and stir it all up together well into a thick paste.

Linseed gruel is a fine tonic for a tired horse. Cook the linseed as for a mash, strain it through muslin to get rid of the grains, and feed the liquid to the horse at once before it turns into jelly.

Linseed jelly is another good tonic that can be added to normal feeds. Cook the linseed very slowly indeed for several hours, stirring at regular intervals to keep it from sticking to the pan, until it has formed into a jelly with about the consistency of starch. Drain away the water which becomes linseed tea and can also be used as a tonic. Linseed soaked in cold water for 24 hours will also jellify in this way.

Oatmeal gruel. Another tonic after a long day. Pour 2 gallons of boiling water, mixed with salt, on to 2 lb. of oatmeal, and serve tepid.

Hay

Good hay should be greenish or light brown in colour; it should be crisp and sweet-smelling without any signs of mustiness or mould. Avoid hay which is either yellow or dark brown, as these colours indicate deterioration. It should be brought when well matured since 'new hay' (in other words that which is less than six months old) tends to be indigestible. The best hay is harvested in early June, when the seed and leaf are at their maximum, and nowadays it is usually sold in bales (rather than trusses). It is far more economical to buy hay by the ton, rather than buying a given number of bales (partly because the latter do not conform to a standard weight).

Horse and Pony Cubes

This is the most recent development in the field of concentrated foods. Several different makes are available but all comprise (in slightly different compositions) a complete balanced ration of hay, corn, molasses and other ingredients which, it is claimed, provides the bulk value of hay as well as the proteins, vitamins, etc.

A hundredweight of these cubes works out a little more expensive than the same quantity, bought separately, of hay and oats to which it is equivalent; on the other hand there is no wastage and also no labour in preparation.

A part ration of hay should be given in addition to the cubes, as much as anything for its occupational value to the horse. No exact quantities can be laid down, since so much depends on the individual animal and the amount of work he is doing, but the following are approximate. A starting ration for, say, a 16 h.h. hunter could be 7 lb. hay plus 15–20 lb. cubes; for a pony, 14.2 h.h., doing light work, not ridden every day, try to begin with 4 lb. hay and 7–8 lb. cubes.

Buying Forage

When buying forage in small quantities do not expect to buy single hundredweights at ton prices. So, when asking a forage merchant for quotations, say exactly the quantity to be supplied, e.g. 1½ cwt. oats, ½ cwt. bran, ½ ton hay, 6 bales of straw.

Prices will inevitably vary, not just according to quality but also between different corn merchants (in the same way that the price of fruit and vegetables will vary from one greengrocer to another). It is therefore worth obtaining several quotations. The names, addresses and telephone numbers of local suppliers can be found in the Telephone Directory's Yellow Pages, under the heading of 'Corn and Agricultural Merchants'.

Stable Management

This term refers comprehensively to the care of the horse or pony whether kept out in a field or in a stable. There will always be arguments as to which is the best thing to do, but in the end it boils down to means and manpower. In either case, the key to success is regular personal observation.

The horse or pony in the paddock needs at least an acre to itself, more if possible. The paddock should be well drained, with healthy grass, free as far as possible from weeds and not sour. A stream of running water along one side is pleasant, but not a pond. The fencing should be good and clear with no wire. Posts and rails are the best, and also the most expensive, but they last longer. A good way of keeping a horse in is by electric fencing; it is safe, economical and flexible, i.e. areas can easily be fenced off in order to rest the ground or to separate belligerent animals.

The field and hedgerows should be free of yew, ivy, and most evergreens, deadly nightshade, hemlock, ragwort, or autumn crocus, which are highly dangerous and often fatal to horses—who don't seem to know it.

A shed or lean-to should be provided facing away from the prevailing wind—three walls and a roof. The horse can be fed there and also have his hay net; grooming can be done there; and it is advisable in the late summer to keep the horse or pony tied up in it during the day to shelter him from flies.

There must be a constant water supply, brought to a proper

trough either through pipe and tap or carried. The presence of the former does not absolve the owner from constant vigilance to see that the supply is maintained.

A lump of rock-salt should always be available in the field for the horse to lick.

Horses and ponies kept out do not as a rule become addicted to the boredom vices of crib-biting and wind-sucking, but they sometimes take great pleasure in chewing the bark off trees, which is why it is not a good thing to keep them in orchards. The only remedy is to paint the tree-trunk with creosote and fence it off in some way.

Whenever possible the horse's droppings should be cleared from the paddock; if left they create sour patches which gradually multiply and ruin the field.

If horses are constantly grazed on any land without its getting any rest or change the dangerous pest of red worm appears, which is very difficult to eradicate. Every year some part of the paddock or grazing area should be fenced off and rested, which is best done by having other animals, cattle, sheep, on it for a while.

Too rich grazing is apt to produce two main troubles: sweet itch and laminitis (fever in the feet). These are most prevalent in ponies. The former is a kind of inflammation of the skin, shown by great irritation, especially round the tail and neck; bare patches appear and the pony rubs itself madly against anything handy. It is seasonal, generally coming on in the late summer, and the only remedy is to take the pony off all green grass and feed it only on dry food. The most convenient and easy food to give would be the various concentrates described above (page 119). Laminitis is the result of too little exercise and too much green food. The remedy is obvious: a prevention rather than cure, the latter being very difficult and by no means certain, unless taken in the very early stages.

A horse or pony left out permanently should generally be left with its natural coat. This, however, creates problems. You must be content with a rough-looking animal, for it is not advisable to groom an outdoor animal as thoroughly as an indoor one. A rubber currycomb will be found invaluable for getting rid of the worst of the mud from a shaggy coat.

If the animal has to do regular fast work, e.g. hunting two or three days a week, and is inclined to sweat a lot, then it had better be clipped and kept out with a New Zealand rug. This is supposed to be unremovable by the horse, but it should be regularly watched all the same.

Catching an outdoor horse or pony is sometimes a problem. It is a good idea to leave head-collars on horses out of doors; if they are habitually difficult to catch, a short length of head rope—about 18 inches—is useful. Apart from that, regular supervision and visiting for other purposes than riding will help to remove the difficulty. The horse or, especially, pony should not feel that every time a human appears it means work.

After hunting, or similar work, an unclipped horse or pony should be turned out as quickly as possible, wet or dry, to be allowed to roll and relax. Examine for possible injuries, cuts, thorns, etc., and then turn him out and place his feed in the shed. A clipped horse must be dried before the New Zealand rug is put on. After a preliminary rub down, cover him with a rug, with some handfuls of straw underneath to absorb the damp. Let him have his feed quietly indoors and then turn him out.

Routine for a stable-kept horse must be adapted to the means available. For an owner-groom, the optimum arrangement would be early morning feed and exercise, grooming, midday feed, evening work and night feed. The main meal will be the midday one, after which the horse should be allowed two hours quietly to digest it. If the horse can have longer time to digest his food you can reduce to two meals a day.

It is possible to streamline and mechanize stable work to some extent. Automatic feeders can be set so as to deliver the previously prepared meal into the manger at the required time in the absence of the owner; automatic watering bowls have long been in use. It is even possible to reduce the inevitable mucking out by the use of mats and porous floors in stables. A little thought in stable planning would enable horses to wander at will from horse-box to exercising paddock and back, thus combining the best of both worlds. The increasing use of concentrated foods can reduce the labour of preparing meals and also ease storage problems.

About Feet

The foot consists of a bony core—the pedal or coffin bone, the navicular (a small wedge-shaped bone which rests across the back of the pedal bone and seems to act as a sort of pulley for the *perforans* tendon), and the short pastern, to which is attached another tendon, the *perforatus*—a highly sensitive laminated cushion, and a hard, insensitive covering of horn.

The fleshy *laminae* are attached to the pedal bone and dovetail into the surrounding horny growth. The sole of the foot is similarly composed of the hard outer sole and a fleshy, sensitive inner sole; the join of the sole and the wall of the hoof is marked by a white line, the appearance of which is the guide to the farrier to stop rasping.

The nails of the shoes must never pierce this white line; if they do they enter the most sensitive part of the foot, causing pain and lameness.

At the back of the foot is the frog, the principal shock absorber, a hard, rubbery wedge-shaped organ, similarly divided into the tough outer covering and the fleshy inner frog. The angles between the wall of the hoof and the sides of the frog are known as the seat of corns, which are inflammations of the sole. Stones and other foreign bodies can get wedged in there and also in the cleft between the two long sides of the frog.

The keeping of the feet clean is one of the most important parts of horse management; it should be a daily job—at least twice, morning and evening, also after work.

The outer horn of the foot grows, like a finger-nail, and in the case of a shod horse has to be kept down artificially, by rasping with a flat file. On no account should the soles or wall of the hoof be cut with a knife, except possibly to remove pieces of dead horn.

The great principle of shoeing is that the shoe must be made to fit the foot, not the foot to fit the shoe. The most heinous fault is dumping, which is cutting the toe to make it fit the shoe instead of obtaining the fit by rasping the sole. It narrows the bearing surface of the foot, exposes the softer layers of the wall, which then become brittle and will not hold the nails.

Shoeing is a whole subject in itself, becoming more important to the owner as the supply of farriers becomes more and more limited. It is impossible to do more than touch on it here and to refer the reader to two useful books: *The Foot and Shoeing*, by Major C. Davenport, O.B.E., F.R.C.V.S. (Pony Club) and *The Principles and Practice of Shoeing*, by Charles M. Holmes, F.W.C.F. (The Farrier's Journal Publishing Co., Ltd.)

Keeping Things Clean

Cleaning tack

Leather, being a natural product (skin) in a specially preserved form, must be fed on grease or oil to live.

When it gets dirty, brush the dirt or mud off, then wipe with a cloth soaked in warm—not hot—water. When nearly dry rub in neatsfoot oil, dubbin (a mixture of fish oil and tallow) or castor oil. If the leather is in contact with clothing, use the 'blended' variety of neatsfoot oil. Good saddle soap has the combined effect of cleaning and preserving, but do *not* use ordinary household soap. When cleaning saddlery of any kind, strip it all into its component parts, and deal with each strap separately, paying special attention to the parts round buckles and strap ends in keepers. Always clean the underside of all straps, etc.

Grease can be removed by rubbing over with a rag moistened with refined benzine.

Dry leather gradually, in a warm room if possible but *never* in front of a fire.

To make new leather really waterproof and supple, the best thing is to saturate it with castor oil and let it soak through in a linen bag to keep the dust off, for at least three months. Occasionally apply more castor oil. In the case of shoes there will be difficulty in polishing at first, but if the oil has thoroughly soaked in and dried off, perseverance will produce better results than without the oil and the shoes or boots will be waterproof for all practical purposes. Saddles and bridles treated like this will have a much longer life. N.B. Do not treat the saddle seat in this way, only straps, flaps, reins, etc.

Always brush the lining of the saddle panels thoroughly before cleaning. Let the sweat dry off numdah pads and saddle blankets before brushing.

Sheepskins can only be brushed dry or dry cleaned. Do not wash them.

Looking After Horses and Ponies on Tour

Horse or pony trekking is a holiday pastime taken up by riders of all ages, and the well-being of mount and man depend entirely on good horsemastership before, during, and after any long-distance ride. These notes are addressed first to owner-riders, but can be applied with advantage by all responsible for holiday rides and tours.

We will begin with the mount, assuming you are going on your own horse or pony (all this also applies to long whole-day rides in the country). He must be fit, so he must have been exercised regularly for at least six weeks before setting out. In particular he must have a saddle and bridle on every day, because if you suddenly took a pony out of a field, put a saddle on him and rode him away for twenty miles, the chances are that he would get a sore back; in any case he would be uncomfortable. When getting him fit I would give him plenty of hay—perhaps a handful of oats mixed with bran and chaff every day, or root vegetables—in addition to ordinary grazing, but see page 116 for the feeding of horses. Give him at least an hour's walk and trot six days a week, increasing to two hours in the last two weeks.

Have the pony shod not less than a week before you start on the trek, which gives him a chance to get his feet comfortable again. It also gives you a chance to see that the shoeing has been properly done—no pricked walls, etc. It is a good idea, too, to get him used to being tethered, as it is better to do that at night in strange places than trying to find the pony in the early morning.

When you go on a trek you usually carry lots of equipment, which may add considerably to the weight to be carried and also may cause discomfort and rubs through swinging feed bags, buckets, etc. Have plenty of rehearsals for carrying kit to make sure that everything is properly fixed to the saddle and does not rattle unnecessarily.

Look to your saddlery. All leather work, bridle, head collar, reins, stirrup leathers, and odd straps, should be thoroughly soft and well impregnated with neatsfoot oil, the bit clean, and make doubly sure that everything fits. Is the padding of the saddle all right? Is the tree off the withers and not pinching them, and not down on the loins? It is a good thing to ride with a blanket under the saddle. A numnah or sheepskin is good, but the blanket has many additional uses on a trek, and that is a good way of carrying it.

The day of your riding holiday dawns, and I hope all the above preparations have been fully carried out. What I say next applies to all ponies, whether your own or provided by the touring organization. First of all, have a final inspection of the saddlery and make last adjustments. Always walk the first mile, then, after a few minutes' trotting, halt, tighten girths and have another look at everything.

You should work out a regular riding routine by the hour, so that you cover five miles in every hour at walk, trot and lead. A pony should trot at from 8–10 m.p.h. and walk at about 4 m.p.h. For leading allow $2\frac{1}{2}$ to 3 m.p.h. So work out the periods each hour at which you should walk, trot, and lead, and keep to that routine all the time. Never, on a tour, try to push your pony beyond his natural speed at every gait. If you want to go further, then you must take more time. With your own pony, you should be able to work out its speeds at the various gaits well in advance. If you are riding in company, of course you must try to accommodate your speed to that of the others, which actually is not very difficult, remembering that it is easier for the faster ponies to go more slowly than to over-press the slower movers. If necessary you can divide into slow and fast groups.

If you are doing twenty miles a day, a long halt after two hours (10 miles) will be ample; if longer, then a short intermediate halt is advisable.

There is not the least harm in breaking the routine by an occasional canter, but do not overdo it, or start it too soon. Let the ponies get well 'run in' first, as one might say. One thing you *must* remember is to change the diagonal at the trot regularly, so that the pony has an equal amount of your weight on each diagonal.

How far should you ride each day? Well, it depends on many factors: fitness, total length of the trek, where the night's lodgings are, etc. But the golden rule is to make the first day's ride a short one—10–15 miles, and for comfort, to try and average not more than 20 miles a day.